Mastering
WordPerfect

Neil J. Salkind

University of Kansas

Merrill Publishing Company
A Bell & Howell Information Company
Columbus Toronto London Melbourne

Published by Merrill Publishing Company
A Bell & Howell Information Company
Columbus, Ohio 43216

This book was set in Century Schoolbook and Eurostyle.

Administrative Editor: Vernon Anthony
Developmental Editor (software): Penelope Semrau
Production Editor: Jeffrey Putnam
Art Coordinator: James Hubbard
Cover Designer: Cathy Watterson

Library of Congress Catalog Card Number: 87-61587
International Standard Book Number: 0-675-20793-2
Printed in the United States of America
    2   3   4   5   6   7   8   9   —   92   91   90   89   88

Contents

Preface

It is more important today than ever before for people who work with information to know something about computers. While there are hundreds of computers and computer programs available, one application seems to stand out among the rest—word processing. This electronic pencil seems to have all but replaced the typewriter and, in doing so, has increased individual and office productivity.

Mastering WordPerfect is an introduction to one such word processing program. WordPerfect has the power and features to satisfy the most demanding user, while it offers a simple and straightforward system of commands that even the novice can understand and learn to use.

Organization of the Book

Mastering WordPerfect has four parts. Part I, *Getting Started: A WordPerfect Tutorial,* introduces the student to the basic features of WordPerfect. After completing this part, the student should be able to use WordPerfect for writing, editing, saving, and printing documents.

Part II, *Advanced WordPerfect,* introduces more advanced features of WordPerfect: using blocks; formatting lines, words, and pages; checking spelling; constructing outlines; and using macros.

Part III, *WordPerfect and Everyday Needs,* reviews some WordPerfect features that are especially useful for home and office needs. This section also includes advice on writing with a word processor and using the word processor to produce well-designed and effective letters.

Part IV, *WordPerfect Extras,* includes ancillary materials for the student. A quick reference chart, a list of all reveal codes and their meanings, a glossary, and a WordPerfect keyboard template help the reader learn and use WordPerfect.

Outstanding Features of the Book

Readability.   Any textbook, especially those that deal with such
technical material as computers and word processing, must communicate ideas and transmit information. This book is carefully
organized through the logical presentation of topics and second-
and third-level headings. This information is presented at a level
that is understandable for the beginning student.

Advance Organizers.   Each lesson begins with a brief list of ob-
jectives detailing what students will know when they read the
chapter and complete the exercises.

Examples.   The book presents examples of WordPerfect features,
with many illustrations. Students are encouraged to participate in
these hands-on exercises; WordPerfect screens show what they
can expect as a result of their efforts.

Important Terms.   At the beginning of each lesson is a list of
the important terms that will appear in that lesson. Each term is
highlighted in the lesson and defined in the glossary at the end of
the book.

Important Keys.   Following the presentation of important terms
is a list of WordPerfect keys and key combinations discussed and
used in the following lesson. While all of these are listed in the
quick reference chart in *WordPerfect Extras,* having them listed
at the front of the lesson informs the student of what keys will be
important in the lesson that follows.

Lesson Exercises.   At the end of each lesson is a set of exercises
that emphasize active use of the lesson's content. Each of these is
designed to get the student to review the materials just learned.

A Note to the Teacher

The software included with this textbook is not a complete version
of WordPerfect, but is only a *training* version developed by the
WordPerfect Corporation especially for this text. It does not have
all the features of the complete version. This will not affect student
learning in any way, since all of the important features (save,
block, delete, spell, etc.) are here. There are two limitations in the
training version: it cannot save documents larger than 50,000
characters, and the student is restricted in the selection of printers
and printer options. The training version will work with most
IBM-compatible printers and other DOS printers, but very technical changes in font styles and pitch, for example, are not supported.

Acknowledgements

Thanks to the reviewers of this book: Joel Levine, Barry University; Dennis Varin, Southern Oregon State University; James

Frankenowski, Lincoln University; Marianne Frey, University of Wisconsin-Superior; John Cuniffe; and Judy Gilboy.

Three people at Merrill deserve a special thanks. Vern Anthony, administrative editor, has been supportive and enthusiastic throughout. Penny Semrau, who played an essential part in discussions with WordPerfect concerning the format of the training version, was always available to help with ideas about content and organization, as well as the technical side of producing the manuscript. Finally, I owe a great deal to Jeff Putnam, who made sure that the manuscript actually became a real book.

Ronda Consolver, Lynne Shapiro and, especially, Bill McCurry worked through the manuscript at various stages and made sure that you really were supposed to push this key rather than that one.

Finally, my family deserves thanks for giving me the time I needed on the third floor and excusing me for the lunches that didn't get made.

N.J.S.

To Sara, on her eleventh birthday

PART I

Getting Started - A Basic Tutorial

- Richard used to spend days retyping the inventory list and changing the purchase order numbers whenever a new product was introduced into the company's line. Now he uses WordPerfect and can change all the numbers in a few hours.

- Susan was very excited about being out on her own, but was anxious about all the work that went along with applying for a job. She didn't even know how to write a letter of introduction or a resume. With some help from library books and WordPerfect, her materials went out in style and the phone calls came in!

- It was certain that no one on the staff was going to volunteer for the job of typing over 1200 *personalized* letters to all the companies that requested literature about the new radio speaker. Besides the letters, envelopes had to be addressed and return labels had to be printed. With WordPerfect, the letters were mailed out within two days.

- When the pension plan was changed, the employee benefits officer needed to write a letter to each of the 1200 employees indicating how the new arrangement would affect his or her future retirement plans. Without WordPerfect, it would have taken several people 3 weeks to do the job. With WordPerfect, the letters arrived full of information and in time for the next meeting, when the various retirement options would be discussed.

LESSON 1
Welcome to WordPerfect

After this lesson you'll know

- Why word processors are so popular.
- What a word processor is and how it can work for you.
- Some dos and don'ts about word processors.
- Some of the things that word processors are used for.
- The difference between input and output.
- The four steps in word processing.

Important Terms

create	merge	save
dictionary	output	speller
edit	print	store
hard copy	retrieve	word processor
input	revise	

The personal computer, like the one you will be using to master WordPerfect, has revolutionized the way people handle information in school, at home, and in the office. Of all the available communication tools, however, none has become more popular than the **word processor.** The word processor has almost replaced the typewriter, and, with its help, you're about to embark on an exciting journey. You'll learn to use the WordPerfect word processing system, a powerful and easy to learn word processor.

How To Use This Book

Mastering WordPerfect is organized into three parts. The first part, *Getting Started - A Basic Tutorial,* is an introduction designed to increase your confidence using the computer and the most important WordPerfect commands. Although many of these commands are basic, they are used in the same way, whether you are typing a one-line memo or a 200-page report.

The second part, *Advanced WordPerfect Techniques,* introduces you to advanced WordPerfect operations including advanced editing, working with files, checking your spelling, doing outlines, and more.

The third part, *Applying WordPerfect,* focuses on how WordPerfect can help you in your everyday writing activities. You will learn about writing effective letters and resumes, doing form letters and tables of contents, and more. This is where all the study you did in parts I and II will pay off handsomely. You will be applying your basic and advanced WordPerfect skills to improve what you can do and how well you do it. Just think of *never* having to retype those 10 pages over again and again, when just one paragraph needs to be changed!

Finally, the last section of the book, *WordPerfect Extras,* contains a glossary, a quick reference card, and more.

To get the most out of *Mastering WordPerfect,* keep in mind the following dos and don'ts.

Some Dos

Do browse through the entire book to get some idea of what material is covered and in what order it is presented. Everything that is covered is important for you to learn.

Do this browsing at your leisure and don't worry about reading each lesson in detail, taking notes, or memorizing the meaning of terms or the location of important keys on the computer keyboard.

As you work through the individual lessons, you'll get a chance to concentrate on detail.

Do read through each *Mastering WordPerfect* lesson before you begin working on your computer. Try to visualize what might happen on the monitor's screen, as it is described in the book. Also, read through the examples and exercises so you can get some idea what you will be expected to do when you begin your hands-on training.

Do follow the directions in each section closely and do exactly what the lesson asks you to do. For example, lesson 4 focuses on entering and saving text. When you are asked, practice this important skill.

Do try the examples as they are presented in the text.

Do keep trying to get the example correct before you move on. While every effort is made to make the examples fail-proof, you might find yourself confused by the material. If this happens, go back to the beginning of the lesson and start over. The lessons in *Mastering WordPerfect* build on each other, so it is important that you master techniques as they are presented.

Do the exercises at the end of each lesson and check your answers with a classmate. You also might want to form a study group to review material and practice using WordPerfect. This way, you can check your work and also help each other generate new ideas about how WordPerfect might be used.

Some Don'ts

Don't fall behind. It is very difficult to catch up.

Don't study or work for too long a time when you first begin to learn WordPerfect. You'll end up tired and frustrated. Instead, work in small chunks of time, giving yourself ample time between work sessions. You know your own pace. One suggestion might be to cover no more than two lessons a day including exercises. Or, try even only one lesson when the lesson involves a large amount of new information.

Don't jump around *Mastering WordPerfect*. Each part of the book is organized in a sequence of lessons that will get you started using WordPerfect. If you want to learn WordPerfect most effectively, follow the lessons in the sequence in which they are presented.

Don't try to learn another word processing program while you are learning WordPerfect. Different programs use different commands and it is easy to become confused and even accidentally erase important information. Learn WordPerfect and then move on to another word processing system. If you already use another word processing system, try to limit the work that you do on the other system while you are learning WordPerfect.

Don't get lazy! Use WordPerfect wherever and whenever you can. When you have other assignments that you can do using WordPerfect, use it! The more you use WordPerfect, the better you will be at word processing.

The Word Processor - Your Electronic Pencil

What is all the fuss about word processors? Imagine, for a moment, writing a letter to a company about a new job and including a copy of your very impressive resume. The next week you get a letter back in the mail agreeing that your credentials are very impressive. However, the company would like the resume reorganized so that work experience comes after, not before, personal experience.

The thought of typing your resume all over again, is so unappealing that you consider dropping the whole thing and possibly losing out on a golden opportunity. With a word processing program like WordPerfect, you could simply identify the portion of your resume you want moved and then move it. In a few keystrokes, you would be finished and still in the running for the job.

A word processor is many different office tools in one. First, it's like a typewriter because it allows you to type memos, letters, and reports quickly and easily. Next, it is like a filing cabinet, allowing you to **store** those memos, letters, and reports where you can **retrieve** them or rearrange them in any order that you want.

Third, it's like having an expert **speller** and a **dictionary** by your side, ready to help you correct whatever misspellings or errors that might come up. Finally, it's like a copying machine. You can print out copy after copy of the same memo or note. You will even learn how to produce customized letters with the same content but different names and addresses.

All of these things can be done with WordPerfect, your computer, a printer, and some practice.

Who Should Use WordPerfect?

The answer is anyone who needs to write, from the president of a company to the person who is responsible for sending out invitations for the holiday party. They have different uses for a word processing system, but they will both find that it saves much time and frustration.

For example, the president could use WordPerfect to generate rough drafts of letters and documents that a secretary would later type and return for signature. The person in charge of the invitations might want to do a draft and show it to others for comments and suggestions. A word processor can make these and other changes very easily.

Some Uses of WordPerfect

The list of things a word processor can do is almost endless. Here are some examples.

- writing memos
- writing a detailed draft of a report that will later be revised
- sending letters
- doing a term paper
- creating a form letter and merging the letter with a list of names and addresses
- creating signs and flyers notifying people about meetings
- transferring information from one document to another
- maintaining mailing lists
- maintaining inventory lists
- designing work schedules
- producing newsletters.

Some of these (such as writing a memo) are easy and straightforward. Others, such as writing form letters and **merging** new information, may involve more steps, but are not necessarily more difficult. *Mastering WordPerfect* will cover all these uses and more.

WordPerfect, and word processors in general, can be invaluable to such fields as law (where long and complex documents are typed), financial institutions (where large volumes of paperwork are processed), schools (where student reports need to be completed and kept on file), health and medicine (where referrals from one physician to another are a regular practice), and any other field where words and ideas are exchanged.

The Four Stages of Word Processing

Before you begin learning about your computer and WordPerfect, let's look at what's involved in word processing (see figure 1-1).

First, the document is **created** by typing the original information into the computer. This is also sometimes called the *input* process.

Second, the document is **saved** so that it can be retrieved or recalled later and revised if necessary. When you save a document, it is also "protected," in case of a power failure or some inadvertent mistake on your part that could cause the destruction of the document and all your hard work. As you will learn later in *Mastering WordPerfect,* it is a good idea to save your work as soon as you are finished with the first draft, or even as you work. Then you have a copy of it to work on later. If you are working on a particularly long paper or project, you may want to save your work every 20 to 30 minutes.

Third, the document is **edited** to correct any mistakes that might have occurred or to make any other changes. Even the best writers, office managers, and word processors don't get the content and typing perfect the first time. Everyone needs to **revise** or edit.

Fourth, when you are satisfied that all the necessary changes have been made, the document can be **printed.** When you print a copy of a document, you produce a **hard copy,** which is a permanent copy of the document. Just as input refers to what you enter into the computer, **output** refers to what the computer produces.

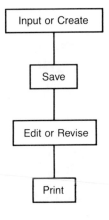

Figure 1–1   The Four Stages in Word Processing

Even after a document is printed, it is often necessary to go back and add additional material and begin the process over again. Although these four separate steps are mentioned in order, you might choose to edit *before* you save your text or print out a copy after the first typing (or inputting). These decisions depend on the way you work and the nature of the project. In general, however, these are the four steps that must take place in order for a document to be properly completed, safely stored, and printed.

LESSON 1 EXERCISES

1. WordPerfect, as well as any word processor, can be used by a variety of people in an organization for many different types of tasks.

   Imagine yourself as the vice president of a large company. In the spaces below write down five different ways that you would use WordPerfect in your everyday work.

   a. _____
   b. _____
   c. _____
   d. _____
   e. _____

2. Along with some of your classmates, write down the features that you think the *perfect* word processor should have. Would it be able to automatically correct spelling errors? Should it be able to automatically underline the same word over and over throughout a report? Should it tell you when you forget to put a verb in a sentence? Grade your spelling? Even write your own reports??!!

3. Ask different faculty members and office workers at your school how they use their word processors. See how many different types of word processors there are and list some of the uses in the spaces below.

   Compare your answers with your classmates'.

   a. _____
   b. _____
   c. _____
   d. _____
   e. _____

4. Go to the library and find an article on word processing. The best places to look are in some of the popular computing magazines, in the *Reader's Guide to Periodical Literature* or newspaper indexes (such as the *New York Times Index* or the *Washington Post Index)*, or in office automation magazines. Write a 200–300 word summary of the article and give your general impression of how valuable this article might be for your classmates to read.

5. What are the four steps involved in word processing?

6. You have just completed an important document that you want to save and add text to when you have more time. Discuss how each of the following terms applies to the additional work you want to do on the document.

   edit   store   output
   revise   speller

7. All word processing programs do basically the same things. Find a friend or a colleague who uses a different program and compare WordPerfect to the other software. What does one do that the other does not? How do they compare in ease of learning? Ease of use? Why would you choose one over the other?

LESSON 2
Your Computer and WordPerfect

After this lesson you'll know

- What system components you need to operate WordPerfect.
- What RAM and K are and why they are important.
- What a disk operating system is and how to operate it.
- The difference between a floppy and a hard disk drive.
- How to set the date and time on your disk operating system.
- How to format a disk.
- What a backup disk is and why it is important.
- How to make a backup disk.
- The parts of the WordPerfect keyboard and what they do.
- Where the function keys are and what they do.
- How to use the WordPerfect template.

Important Terms

backup disk	format	random access
clone	function keys	memory (RAM)
compatible	hard disk	read
cursor	input	retrieved
cursor keys	K	software
disk drive	monitor	system level
disk operating system	number pad	template
(DOS)	personal computer (pc)	24 hour clock
file	printer	write
floppy disk	prompt	

Important Keys

Alt   Ctrl   Shift
Back Space

The **personal computer** in front of you looks like a typewriter with a television set on top of it. You may know little about this electronic marvel; you may not know how it works or what you are supposed to do with it.

Take heart. Using a personal computer is no more difficult than starting your car or using a hand calculator. All it takes is patience. The personal computer you will use to learn WordPerfect is probably an IBM computer or a **clone**, manufactured by such companies as Zenith, Kaypro, Leading Edge, Tandy, or Compaq. A clone is a computer that can operate, or is **compatible** with, another type of computer and can use the same **software**. Most of the available clones are IBM clones.

What You Need To Use WordPerfect

In order to use WordPerfect, your computer needs at least the following components:

- An IBM, or an IBM-compatible, computer that has at least 256K of RAM. A **K** (short for kilobyte) is a measure of storage, with 1K equal to approximately 1,000 characters. In other words, a page that is 50 spaces wide and 20 lines long would take up about 1K worth of memory space. **RAM** or **random access memory** is the amount of space your computer has available for everyday work tasks. It is not permanent storage space, but is available only when the computer is operating. When the computer is turned off, everything stored in RAM disappears. It's like erasing the writing on a chalkboard. To store things permanently, the information in RAM is transferred to another storage medium such as a **floppy** or a **hard disk**.

- At least one floppy disk, which looks like a phonograph record or a circular platter inside a protective sleeve. Floppy disks are made of the same flexible magnetic material as a cassette tape. A hard disk is made of rigid magnetic material. While a hard disk can store much more information than a floppy disk and works *much* faster, it is also more expensive and often subject to mechanical problems. WordPerfect version 4.2, the word processing software that you use, comes on a floppy disk.

● A floppy **disk drive**. A floppy disk drive is the device that "spins" the floppy disk and **reads** information on the disk into your computer's RAM, or allows new information to be **written** on the disk from your computer's RAM. If you have only one disk drive, it is usually referred to as drive A. If you have two disk drives, one will be referred to as A and one will be referred to as B. More about this later.

Most of the instructions in *Mastering WordPerfect* will be for systems with two disk drives. In two-disk-drive systems, one disk drive reads commands off the WordPerfect disk. The other (disk drive B) operates the disk on which the documents you produce will be stored. Figure 2–1 shows how disk drives can be arranged.

If the two drives are arranged next to each other, the one on the left is drive A and the one on the right is drive B. If the two drives are stacked with one upon the other, then the A drive is usually on the top and the B drive on the bottom.

● A **disk operating system** (often called **DOS**), provided on a floppy disk that came with your computer. The operating system instructs the computer how to perform various tasks. It is the bridge between you and WordPerfect.

The operating system is usually contained on a single disk labeled MS-DOS (for MicroSoft disk operating system) or PC-DOS (for personal computer disk operating system). Both of

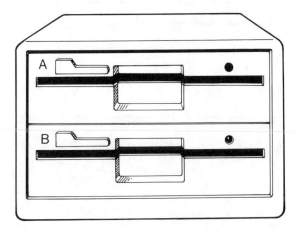

Figure 2–1   Floppy Disk Drives A and B

these will operate WordPerfect. There are other operating systems that will work as well.

- A **printer**, a necessary part of any word processing system. While a printer is not necessary for learning how to use WordPerfect, you will probably want to produce copies of your documents.

- Finally, a **monitor** connected to your computer. WordPerfect works beautifully in color, but it is not necessary to have a color monitor. A monochrome (black and white, green, or amber) will do just fine.

Starting Your Computer: The Disk Operating System

All computers have their own disk operating system. This is the computer's internal set of directions that controls its operations. The first step in using WordPerfect is to start the computer using the disk operating system. To do this, follow these steps.

1. Find the floppy disk that contains the disk operating system (DOS) and place it into disk drive A, as shown in figure 2–2. When the disk containing the operating system is in drive A, close the disk drive door. It should catch and remain shut.

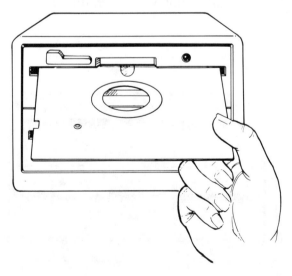

Figure 2–2   Inserting the DOS Disk

2. Turn on your computer and your monitor. After a short period of time and a possible beep from your computer (depending upon the type of computer you have), the first thing you will see on your monitor is

> Current date is Tue 1-01-1980
> Enter new date:

WordPerfect Hint

Most computers that use MS or PC-DOS ask you for date (and time) information in the way you see above. But, not all computers that can use WordPerfect display the information in exactly the same way. What's important is that they request the same information, but in a different form.

Your DOS system wants you to provide today's date, entered as the number of the month (from 1 to 12), the number of the day (from 1 to 31), and the last two digits of the year. For example, May 2, 1987 would be entered as 05-02-87 or 5-2-87 and December 16 would be entered as 12-16-87.

After entering the date, press the return key. If you make an error entering the date, simply use the **backspace** key to move backwards to erase the error.

Why does DOS want the date? Part of the operating system keeps track of what you do on your computer. Part of this keeping track is noting the date that a **file** is created. A file is a separate and unique collection of information, much like a folder in a file cabinet. Just as folders are stored in file cabinets, files are stored on disks.

Entering the date helps you keep track of your WordPerfect files, including when they were first started.

WordPerfect Hint

Although personal computers are marvelous machines, they can do only what they are told. They follow instructions very well, but the instructions must be clear. Because you give the computer instructions, you must make sure that throughout Mastering WordPerfect *you enter directions exactly as they appear in the book. Include things like spaces and commas as they are required.*

After you enter the date, press the return key. DOS will then show the current time and request the new time:

Current time is 0:00:25.35
Enter new time:

Enter the time with the hours, minutes, and seconds, separated by colons and a period. DOS uses a **24 hour clock**, so anything after noon has 12 hours added to it. For example, ten-thirty in the morning should be entered as 10:30:00.00 or more simply 10:30. Five minutes and 27 seconds past two in the afternoon should be entered as 14:05.27.00 or more simply 14:05.27.

Notice how DOS already shows some time even before you are asked to supply a new time. That's because the DOS clock begins as soon as the operating system is loaded, not when you enter the time. When you enter the time, the clock begins again at that new starting point.

After entering the current time, press the return key and you should see the A prompt as A>. The capital A tells you that you are operating in drive A. The A (or the B if you were on disk drive B) is a **prompt**, a signal that you are at the operating **system level** and that the computer is asking you to supply some information.

You are now ready to use your computer to make a backup copy of your WordPerfect disk.

WordPerfect Hint

DOS lets you reset the time and date at any time if you are still at the system level, the level you are at when you see the A prompt. You can tell that you are at the system level when you see a prompt, such as A> or B>, as the last thing on your monitor. If you want to reset the date or the time, just type in "date" or "time" and you will be asked to enter the current date or time. This can be handy if you either forget to enter the date or time or enter it incorrectly. But remember, you can only do this at the system level.

Making a Backup Disk

Working with a computer, and especially doing word processing, can be enjoyable and time saving. But, as with any other skill, there are certain practices that you should learn and use whenever necessary. One of these practices is making a **backup disk** of your original WordPerfect disk.

What is a backup disk? A backup disk is an exact copy of your original disk. In your everyday WordPerfect training and exercises you will use the backup disk and not the original.

What happens to the original or master disk that came with this book? Store it in a safe place and use it only if something on your backup disk is destroyed or, for some reason, does not work properly. The backup disk is insurance and, if copied properly, should be just as good as the original.

Formatting a Disk

Before you make a backup of your original WordPerfect disk, you must first prepare, or **format**, a blank floppy disk so that the individual files on the WordPerfect disk can be transferred to the backup.

Formatting a disk separates it into sectors and tracks; this allows DOS to keep a record of where things are located. This is very important when it comes time to **retrieve** a saved file.

To format a new disk, follow these steps.

1. If you have not already, place your DOS disk in drive A (the top one or the left one, as shown in figure 2–2). Close the disk drive door.

2. Type in the following command: A>format b: <ret>. This command requests that the formatting operation begin, and that the disk to be formatted be the one in disk drive B. The <**ret**> means press the return (or enter) key. After a moment, you will see the following message on your screen:

    > Insert new diskette for drive B:
    > and strike enter when ready__

When you press the enter key, you will see the red lights go on for both the A and B disk drives and the formatting process will begin. Don't be impatient. It takes a few minutes for the entire formatting process to be completed.

WordPerfect Hint

When a disk is formatted, all of the information that was previously on that disk is erased. It is as if you are starting with a new disk. Be careful and make sure that you are using either a new disk or one that has information on it you no longer need.

3. When the new disk is formatted, you may be asked to provide
    a name for it. Type in **wrdpf** (for WordPerfect), and hit the
    return key. Some versions of DOS do not ask for such a name.
    You now have a newly formatted disk, named "wrdpf," that is
    still in disk drive B.

    DOS will then give you some information about the
    amount of space that is available on the disk and will ask you
    whether you want to format another disk. Press the "n" key for
    no and you will be returned to the A> prompt.

Making the Backup

Once the blank disk is formatted, you are ready to continue making a backup of the original WordPerfect disk. To complete the
backup procedure, follow these steps.

1. Remove the DOS disk from disk drive A.

2. Take your original WordPerfect disk and place it in disk drive
    A. Close the disk drive door. The newly formatted disk should
    now be in drive B and you should have a disk in each drive.
    The original WordPerfect disk should be in drive A, and the
    newly formatted disk should be in drive B.

3. Type in the following command: A>copy a:*.* b:*.* <ret>.
    This command copies each of the individual files from the disk
    in drive A on to the blank disk in drive B. The stars (*) are
    part of the operating system's commands. As the copying takes
    place, you will see the name of each file being listed. The pro-
    cess is finished when the message on your screen tells you that
    three files were copied and the A> prompt appears again.

4. Remove the disks from the disk drives.

5. Place the original WordPerfect disk in a safe place where it is
    not in any danger of being damaged from handling or heat.

6. Take one of the labels that come with your box of blank disks
    and write "wrdpf" on it. Place the label on the backup disk. It's
    a good idea to do any writing on disk labels *before* the label is
    placed on the disk so that sharp writing instruments will not
    damage the actual disk. Many people use a felt tip pen to min-
    imize the possibility that the disk will be damaged.

    Congratulations, you have just copied your original Word-
Perfect disk onto another disk and are ready to continue with your
WordPerfect training.

Your Computer Keyboard and WordPerfect

As with any other software program, pressing certain keys on your keyboard begins certain WordPerfect operations. There are the letters and numbers that are used for actual data and text **input**, but other special purpose keys are just as important.

The goal of any well-designed computer program, and especially a well-designed word processing program, is to have the keys arranged so two things are accomplished.

First, keys that do the same general things should be grouped together. This allows you to move quickly from one operation to another. On many personal computers, the **function keys** (*F1, F2, F3,* and so on) on the left side of the keyboard form the first group. These keys may also be located across the top of the keyboard.

The second set of important special keys is the **cursor keys** located on the right side of the keyboard, including the **number pad**. The cursor keys control the movement of the **cursor**, which is the little flashing light that helps you keep track of where you are on your screen.

These sets of keys are highlighted in figure 2–3.

You will learn to use the function keys and the cursor keys to control everything except the actual entry of text, such as letters, words, symbols, and numbers. As you continue with your Word-Perfect training, you will see what type of operation each of the function and the cursor keys performs.

WordPerfect Hint

Some computers have the function and cursor keys in different positions from those described in figure 2–3. For example, on some models, the function keys are placed across the top of the keyboard. No matter what their location, they accomplish the same thing.

The WordPerfect Function Keys and Template

WordPerfect places special importance on the 10 function keys. Alone, and in combination, these are used to perform every major operation in WordPerfect. In fact, each of these keys actually can perform *four* different functions.

First, when they are pressed alone, they perform a specific WordPerfect function. But, depending on which function key and

Figure 2–3   The Function Keys and the Cursor Keys

combination of one of the three other keyboard keys is pressed, other operations are performed. These three other important keyboard keys are the *control* key (marked **Ctrl** on the keyboard), the *shift* key (marked **Shift** or, as in figure 2-3 with an arrow), and, the *alternate* key (marked **Alt**), all shown in figure 2–3.

You can see on your keyboard (and in figure 2–3) that these keys are in a certain order, with the Ctrl key at the top, the Shift key in the middle, and the Alt key on the bottom. WordPerfect offers you a summary of these functions shown in figure 2–4. Each

F1	Cancel	**Spell** ← *SEARCH* Replace Search →	F2
F3	**Screen** *SWITCH* Reveal Codes Help	**Move** → *INDENT* ← Block → Indent	F4
F5	*DATE* Mark Text List Files	**Tab Align** *CENTER* Flush Right Bold	F6
F7	*PRINT* Math/Columns Exit	**Print** *LINE FORMAT* Page Format Underline	F8
F9	**Merge/Sort** *MERGE E* Merge Codes Merge R	**Macro Def.** *RETRIEVE TEXT* Macro Save Text	F10

Legend

Ctrl + Function Key
SHIFT + FUNCTION KEY
Alt + Function Key
Function Key alone

Figure 2–4   Summary of WordPerfect Function Keys

of these keys, in combination with one of the 10 function keys, will begin a different WordPerfect operation.

To make using these keys and key combinations easy, a **template** has been designed that fits around the function keys on your keyboard and acts as a constant reminder of what keys and what key combinations perform what operations. This template is supplied with this book. Place it on the keyboard as in figure 2–5. The training version template offers many, but not all, of these options.

When the template is in place, you can see that beside each of the function keys is a list of the different operations that can be performed using either the function key alone, or using it in combination with one of the other three keyboard keys.

For example, when you want to exit or leave WordPerfect you

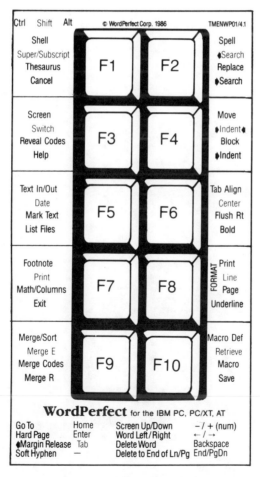

Figure 2–5   WordPerfect Template Installed on the Keyboard

would press only the F7 function key. If you wanted to begin the spelling function, you would hold the Ctrl key down and press the F2 key. If you wanted to print out a hard copy of you work, you would hold the Shift key down and press the F7 key.

But which of the three keyboard keys should you press? As you can see in figure 2–4, you always press Ctrl if you want to perform the operation that is listed first (from the top) on the template. The *Shift* key is pressed for the second operation, and the *Alt* key for the third operation. If you want to perform the fourth function listed, then pressing the function key alone is sufficient.

Almost all WordPerfect learners rely upon the template to remind them of what combination of keys accomplishes what. Fairly soon, however, if you practice, you'll find that you need to rely less on the template, since the definition of the keys and their use will become so routine that you'll hardly think about it at all.

LESSON 2 EXERCISES

1. What is a disk operating system?
   What is the name of the disk operating system that you are using?
   Why is a disk operating system important?
   How do you know if you are at the system level when you begin working on your computer?
   Why can't you use any disk operating system on any computer?

2. What are some of the precautions you need to take when working with floppy disks?
   What is the difference between a floppy and a hard disk?

3. Here are some times and dates. Write down what you would type if you were entering them.
   March 3, 1986   _____
   December 3, 1985   _____
   11/10/84   _____
   29 March, 1947   _____
   ten-thirty AM   _____
   two minutes past noon _____
   five past six at night _____

4. Why is it important to enter the date and the time when you first enter the operating system?

5. Your computer probably has two disk drives. Which is the A drive and which is the B drive?
   Why is it important to know the difference between the two?
   In a two-disk-drive system, what function does drive A play?
   What function does drive B play?

6. What is RAM and what is a "K"?
   Why is it important in storing a document?

7. What is a backup and why is it important to make one?
   What is a write protect sticker, and when would you use one?

8. List all the steps that are necessary in making a backup disk, including formatting the disk that will be used as the backup.

9. What is the difference between the original master disk and a backup disk?

10. Why does the original or master disk need to be stored in a safe place?

11. What is the difference between the function keys and the cursor keys?

     Why are all the function keys and the cursor keys located so close to each other?

LESSON 3
Starting WordPerfect

After this lesson you'll know:

- How to start WordPerfect.
- What information the WordPerfect opening screen contains.
- What a default value is.
- What the document indicator is and why it is important.
- What the page indicator is and why it is important.
- What the line position indicator is and why it is important.
- What the character position indicator is and why it is important.
- What a split screen is and why it is important to WordPerfect.

Important Terms

character position indicator	line indicator	tab key
default	page indicator	tab
document indicator	split screen	

You are now ready to begin using WordPerfect, an exciting moment for a first time word processor like yourself! First, a brief review. You should have a copy of your WordPerfect program disk in the A drive of your computer and a blank formatted disk in the B drive of your computer. The computer should be turned on, and you should be at the system level, where the monitor screen should be showing the A prompt. (A>).

Even though you will not be dealing with the data disk (the one in drive B) during this part of *Mastering WordPerfect,* it's a good idea to get used to this arrangement, since you will eventually learn to save all of your files on disk B. It will be important to save your files on to the data disk, since most of disk A is already filled with WordPerfect program files and there is little spare room to store your newly created documents as files.

Starting the WordPerfect Program

Starting WordPerfect is as easy as typing in the two letters wp and pressing the return key like this: A>wp <ret> Do this now. When you are done, the red light in drive A should come on, indicating that the disk drive is working. A short time later, you should see the welcoming screen shown in the top screen of figure 3–1.

The WordPerfect Welcoming Screen

The developers of WordPerfect have created several different versions of this word processing program. If you are using this book in a school class, you have received a training version, which was developed with the particular needs of the beginning word processing student in mind.

As you can see on the opening screen shown in figure 3–1, there are several disclaimers that most software developers want the user to read and understand.

The first indicates that this version of WordPerfect is copyrighted and protected under the appropriate laws. This means that this program and its contents cannot be copied and sold by anyone other than the developers of WordPerfect. The second reemphasizes this by telling you that you can copy and use WordPerfect for demonstration and training, but not for any other reason (such as making copies and giving them to friends). This stipulation allows you to make a backup, but does not allow you to let anyone else use

```
                    ┌─────────────────────────┐
                    │                         │
                    │      WordPerfect        │
                    │                         │
                    ├─────────────────────────┤
                    │      Version 4.2        │
                    └─────────────────────────┘

              (C)Copyright 1982,1983,1984,1985,1986
                      All Rights Reserved
                    WordPerfect Corporation
                        Orem, Utah  USA




        NOTE: The WP System is using A:




        * Please Wait *
```

```
                    WordPerfect 4.2 -- Training Version
                    Copyright 1986 WordPerfect Corporation


        This special training version is        The training version of
        provided to help you get to know         WordPerfect has been limited in
        WordPerfect.  It is protected by         the following ways:
        Federal Copyright Law and
        international trade agreements.        * Saved documents are limited in
                                                 size to about 50,000
        You are allowed to copy and use          characters;
        this software for demonstration
        and training purposes.  You are        * Printed output is limited to
        not allowed to use copies of the         one page and occasionally
        software, in whole or in part,           contains "*WPC";
        for any other purpose.
                                               * Advanced printing features are
        WordPerfect Corporation retains          not allowed;
        title to the software.
                                               * LPT1 (PRN) is the only port
                                                 that can be used for printing.


                    Press any key to continue
```

Figure 3–1   The WordPerfect Opening Screen

that backup or the original disk. Finally, WordPerfect Corporation, the developers and manufacturers of WordPerfect, retain the title to the software.

The training version of WordPerfect contains all of the same capabilities of its big sister, the original WordPerfect word processing program. Because it was designed to fit on only one disk (instead of five like its sibling), there are a few limitations on how much it can do. For example, files created on your training version cannot be read by the commercial version of WordPerfect, and vice versa. Also, your printed copies of materials might sometimes contain the letters "*WPC," standing for WordPerfect Corporation.

Now that you have been officially welcomed, it's time to move on and begin using WordPerfect. Press any key and look for the opening WordPerfect screen.

The WordPerfect Opening Screen

Beginning to write with a word processor is just like typing on a clean sheet of paper. Figure 3–1 shows the opening WordPerfect screen, blank and ready for you to type on. You will enter some text in the next lesson, but before you do,there are some important indicators on the screen.

The Document Indicator

One of WordPerfect's practical features is that it lets you look at more than one document at a time *on the same screen*. You can actually split the screen into two parts (which you will do in lesson 15).

For example, you might be writing a memo to an employee on one part of the screen, while copying a list of suggestions from a handbook from another part of the same screen. Both of these documents can be shown simultaneously on a **split screen.**

When you begin to use windows you must have some way to keep track of which document you are working on. Even though you can see two documents at once, you can only work on one at a time. When you are working on document 1, the first indicator at the bottom of the screen, the **document indicator,** will say "Doc 1." If you were working on document 2, the first indicator at the bottom of the screen would say "Doc 2."

Figure 3–2 shows you a completed screen containing a letter. You can see that the document indicator is on "Doc 1."

```
April 2, 1986

Dear Phil,

I'm happy to inform you that the plans for the annual banquet are
coming along quite well. As of today, we have 105 people who
have made reservations and have sent in their registration fee.

I was wondering if you could please help us with some of the last
minute arrangements. Our guest speaker, Dr. Elhod, needs to be
picked up at the airport at 5 PM on the day of the banquet. If
you could do that, I would really appreciate it. Please call me
if you need any more information. Call me at home or at work.

Thank you,


                                 Doc 1  Pg 1  Ln 13    Pos 48
```

Figure 3–2   A WordPerfect Letter with the Cursor at Document 1, page 1, line 13, and position 48

The Page Indicator

The next indicator, the **page indicator,** is used to tell you what page (Pg) of a document you are currently working on. Right now, as in figure 3–2, it is page 1.

The Line Indicator

Besides the document and the page, it is important for you to know what line (Ln) you are working on. This allows you to know when a new page will come. It's also a handy number to know when planning such things as where figures and charts should be inserted.

The line indicator is also the first of these four markers that deals with the position of the cursor. Remember, the cursor is the blinking symbol that lets you know exactly where you are on the current page. As you can see in figure 3–3, the cursor is located on line 13.

The Character Position Indicator

Finally, the column number or **character position indicator** (Pos), where the cursor is located, is indicated in the lower right hand corner of the screen. This number is useful for such things as setting **tabs** (or places where the cursor stops when the **Tab key** is pressed), new margins, and general spacing requirements. In figure 3–3, the cursor is located in column 48 on the *m* in the word *home*.

When the cursor is on the far left side of the screen, the number showing in the position indicator is equal to the setting for the left hand margin. In this case, the **default** (or the pre-set value) for the lefthand margin is 10.

If you are using a color monitor, you will see a change in the character position indicator as certain WordPerfect options, such as underlining text, **bolding text,** and the **combination** of the two, are used.

Now that you know how to determine where you are in a document, it's time to move on to the next lesson, where you will enter and work with text by writing a simple memo.

WordPerfect Hint

Many of the lessons in Mastering WordPerfect *require you to begin the lesson with a clear screen. If at any time you want to leave WordPerfect, press the F7,N,Y combination of keys. (These are three separate keystrokes and you* do not type the commas.) *You will then be returned to the A prompt. You'll learn more about leaving WordPerfect in lesson 7.*

LESSON 3 EXERCISES

1. What two-letter command is used to start WordPerfect? What drive should the WordPerfect disk be inserted into to begin using the program?

2. What is the difference between the training version of Word-Perfect and the regular version of WordPerfect? How will these differences affect the kind of work that you can do?

3. Why is a data disk used in word processing? How does a data disk differ from a program disk?

4. In the following paragraph, what are the actual values of the line and character positon indicators for the *i* in the word *in* at the end of the fourth line?

    > There is no difference between the two types of school programs, except for the fact that one starts earlier in the morning. For parents who both work and may need the extra time, the one that starts earlier in the day might be better.

5. In the above paragraph, what letter would the cursor be on if the values of the line and character position indicators were *Ln 2 Pos 8?*

6. What should the document, page, line, and position indicators show when you begin a new WordPerfect document?

7. Write out five ways that the document, page, line, and cursor indicators might be important to your wordprocessing activities.

    a. _____

    b. _____

    c. _____

    d. _____

    e. _____

8. Name three ways that you would use a split screen in Word-Perfect.

9. What four indicators are shown in the WordPerfect opening screen? Explain what each one does and how it is used in WordPerfect.

LESSON 4:
Entering and Saving Text

After this lesson you'll know

- What word wrap is and why it is important to word processing.
- How text is entered in WordPerfect.
- What an extension is and how it is used.
- How you can use extensions to help manage your files.
- How to name files.
- How to rename a file.
- How to save text.
- When text should be saved.

Important Terms

extension	label	save
file name	margins	word wrap

Important Keys

F1	F10

Finally, it's time to begin writing some text and working with other WordPerfect features. At this point you should still have a blank WordPerfect screen (you have yet to type anything on it), with the blinking cursor located at the upper left corner of the screen. If you have accidentally typed on your screen, see the Quick Reference Card at the back of this book for instructions on clearing your screen.

Word Processors and Typewriters

Before you begin entering your first words and sentences, there are certain things you need to know about the typing and WordPerfect.

Word Wrap

The first is that WordPerfect (as do many other word processors) has a convenient feature called **word wrap.** Word wrap allows you to continue typing without worrying about where the current line will end or if you will remember to press the return key when you get to the end of a line (as with a conventional typewriter).

In other words, the words actually wrap around and automatically continue on the next line. You will not get awkward extended single lines like the one shown in figure 4–1. So when you type a memo, watch the right hand margin as it adjusts to the word that is typed and places it on the next line if it is too long.

Unless you tell WordPerfect to do so, it will not break up words and insert hyphens.

Paragraphing

You need to press the return key only when you want to begin a new paragraph.

The number of words that can be typed on any one line depends, of course, on how long the line length is set at (you'll learn to do this in lesson 14). Line length depends entirely on **margins** settings. A margin is the blank space on the left or the right hand side of the page. The default margin settings for a WordPerfect document are 10 spaces for the left hand margin and 74 spaces for the right hand margin.

In the second part of *Mastering WordPerfect,* you'll learn how to change these margins to accommodate the type of document you are creating.

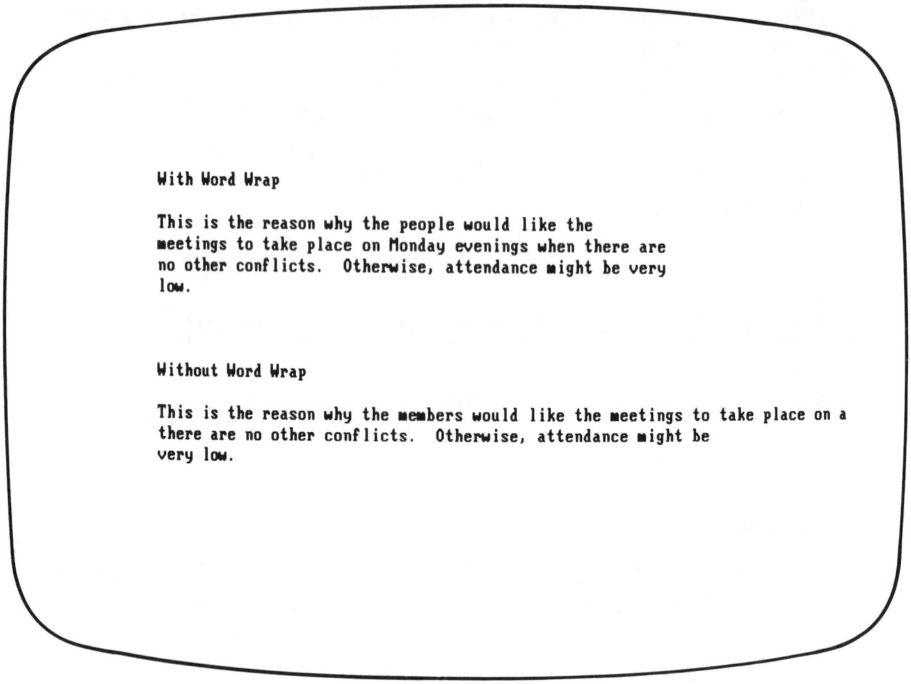

```
With Word Wrap

This is the reason why the people would like the
meetings to take place on Monday evenings when there are
no other conflicts.  Otherwise, attendance might be very
low.


Without Word Wrap

This is the reason why the members would like the meetings to take place on a
there are no other conflicts.  Otherwise, attendance might be
very low.
```

Figure 4–1   Some Text with and without Word Wrap

Writing a Simple Memo

Maybe you thought the time to actually write would never come, but now it's here!

Figure 4–2 is a memo announcing a departmental meeting. Type the entire memo *exactly* as it appears, *including all of the errors*. Remember that you only need to press the return key at the end of each paragraph. Otherwise, WordPerfect's word wrap will do the work for you.

Mistakes are intentionally included in this memo so that you can practice correcting them later. Learning how to correct errors is a major part of learning to use a word processor. Although this is a simple exercise, you will be doing exactly the same things that are done no matter how long or how complex a document might be.

Type in the document now.

Saving Text

Before you begin learning how to correct the four types of errors in this memo, you must first **save** the document as a file. The save

```
                            MEMO
        August 15, 1986

        To: All division heads

        From: Vcie-president Nicholas

        There will be be a meting of the entire administrative group at
        10 A.M. on Thursday, September 4, 1986 in my office.  Please
        bring yourrecommendations for employee of month with you to this
        meeting.

        Thank you and I look forward to seeing you all on the 4th.
```

Figure 4–2   Departmental Memo with Errors

step (as shown in figure 1–1) ensures that you have a copy of it on your disk.

Why should you practice saving a file before it is entered exactly as you want it? It's a matter of being safe rather than sorry. One of the most important features of any word processing program is its ability to save the work you have already completed, so you can recall and work on it later.

When you are working on a document, (before it is saved for the first time), the only "copy" of it is stored in the memory (remember RAM?) of the computer. If, for some unforeseen reason, the computer should malfunction or the power (and the computer) go off, whatever is stored in this temporary memory will be lost. It literally disappears, whether it is a one-line letter or a ten-page report. *Save documents as you work!*

Learning to save a document will be your introduction to using function and keyboard keys in combination to perform some of the WordPerfect's most basic (and often most important) features. In order to save a memo such as the one you have on your current screen as a file, you must first, however, give it a name.

Naming Files

If you wanted to find a book in the library, you would probably begin by looking in the card catalogue under the title of the book. The book has a **label** attached to it that, most importantly, no other book shares. In other words, the label or name of the book is unique.

It's the same way with any document you want to save with WordPerfect. You must assign a unique **file name** to it. For example, if you were to name a file "letter", you might find it confusing since you will surely be writing more than one letter.

WordPerfect won't let you assign the same name to two different files. If you had two files with the same name, how would you know which of your many letters is the one to your division head thanking her for the raise and which is a letter of warning to an employee who has many unexcused absences? That could be embarrassing!

Also, even though you might have a unique name for your files (such as "divhead" and "employ"), you might not be able to remember what general type of document your file represents.

It's for this reason that you not only want to name a file something that hints at its content (such as whom it is written to in the case of a letter), but you might also want to use what is called an **extension,** which reflects the general category of the file.

For example, the memo that you saw in an earlier *Mastering WordPerfect* lesson (see figure 3–3), was addressed to Phil. One informative and easy-to-recognize file name would be "phil". But, since you may want to distinguish it from a report, you might want to attach the extension "ltr" following the name "phil".

File names can be up to 8 characters long. Extensions can be up to 3 characters long, should have no spaces, and must follow the file name and a period. The entire name of the document would then be "phil.ltr".

WordPerfect Hint

The operating system (DOS) that WordPerfect uses allows only certain symbols (and all letters and numerals) to be used in the names of files. These are

! @ # $ % & ( ) _- { } '

For example, a letter to Susan might be named "susan.ltr", a memo to the garage might be named "garage.mem", and a final report on the Williams project might be named "Williams.rpt".

Remember that you have to keep your file names straight if you are going to know what document to recall later. Imagine having a whole set of files named "letter1", "letter2", "letter3", and so on. Here is a list of possible extensions that you might want to use.

WordPerfect Hint

General Category	Extension
memo	mem
letter	ltr
report	rpt
list	lst

Saving the Memo

Here comes your first exercise using function keys. In order to save the document that is currently active (i.e., the one you just entered), press F10, which is the last of the function keys. The F10 key alone begins the WordPerfect Save operation.

When you press the F10 key, a new line will appear at the bottom left hand corner of the screen that reads

Document to be Saved:

What WordPerfect now wants is a name so it can assign that name to the file and save it on a disk for permanent storage. The name of this file will be "divhead.mem". Type in that file name now.

As you can see in figure 4–3, that name has been typed in (including the period between the file name and the extension).

When you press the return key, the next message you should see is

Saving A:\divhead.mem

If WordPerfect could talk, it would be telling you "I am saving your file named 'divhead.mem' on the disk in drive A."

WordPerfect can't talk, but it does the next best thing. After the first save, the following message will appear:

A:\divhead.mem

in the lower left hand corner of the screen. It will display the name of the file and the active disk drive.

Knowing what file you are working in is very important and helps you keep track of your different documents. If you do not want this message displayed on the monitor screen, you can eliminate it using the set-up menu discussed in part 4 of this book.

Don't forget, you have another disk drive that WordPerfect

```
                              MEMO
August 15, 1986

To: All division heads

From: Vcie-president Nicholas

There will be be a meting of the entire administrative group at
10 A.M. on Thursday, September 4, 1986 in my office.  Please
bring yourrecommendations for employee of month with you to this
meeting.

Thank you and I look forward to seeing you all on the 4th.




Document to be Saved: A:\divhead.mem
```

Figure 4–3   Departmental Memo with Errors and Save Line

could have saved the file to as well. The reason that WordPerfect saved the file to drive A is that the A drive is the one that WordPerfect automatically saves to unless told otherwise. In other words, disk drive A is the default drive.

WordPerfect Hint

At any time if you get into trouble while learning WordPerfect, press the F1 key. This will cancel the operation and get back to the active document. You can't hurt your document by pressing the **F1** *key. This is your bail-out key! Use it when you really need to.*

Congratulations again! You have just saved a memo. At any time, you will be able to recall that memo and work on it, as, in fact, you will do in the next lesson.

LESSON 4 EXERCISES

1. How does word wrap work and why does it make word processing easier?

2. What is a unique file name? Why is it important to use them? In the space provided below, provide some examples of documents and the file names that you would attach to them.

File Type (letter, etc.)	File Name
letter	sara.ltr
memo	mechanic.mem
recipe	quiche.yum
_____	_____
_____	_____
_____	_____
_____	_____

3. Which of the following file names are not very useful and why?
   bill james.draft1
   .scott
   james.ltr
   james.letter
   wilson. government report
   scott.mem

4. Which of the following file names are unsuitable? Why?
   bill.letter
   final report.doc
   .123
   professional.form
   bill,mike.ltr

5. Why is saving a file important? How often should you save a file? Why?

6. What is the difference between a file name and an extension? What are some general extensions that you might use in your school or business activity?

7. How do you rename a file? When should you do this?

8. Enter the following brief paragraph:

   This is the beginning of a course that will teach you how to use a very popular word processor. If you take the time to practice, you will learn how to use this valuable tool.

   a) Save this paragraph as a file under the name "exer6.1".

   b) Now create another copy of this paragraph exactly as typed, by saving it under a new name "exer6.2".

   c) Finally, change the word *tool* to *software program*. Now save it under the filename "exer6.2".

9. What is the exact sequence of keys you need to press in order to save a newly created document? What sequence is needed to "resave" a document that has already been created and has been saved at least once?

LESSON 5
Editing Text: Nobody's Perfect!

After this lesson you'll know

- Why everyone needs to edit first, second, and even more drafts!
- How to use the cursor keys on the right-hand side of the keyboard.
- How to delete letters and words using the backspace key.
- How to insert letters and words using the insert option.
- About the most frequent kinds of errors people make in entering text: the *reversal, runon, double type double type,* and speling errrors.
- The importance of saving your document after changes are made.

Important Terms

back space key	direction arrows	reversal
control key	edit	typeover mode
cursor control keys	insert mode	
delete key	replace	

Important Keys

Ctrl/Back Space	Down arrow	Ins
Del	F10	Up arrow

Whether you want to change one letter, one word, one sentence, or an entire paragraph, you'll welcome the ease with which you and WordPerfect can **edit** a document. *Everybody* needs to edit his or her documents. Learning how to make the necessary changes quickly and efficiently is one of the keys to being a good WordPerfect user. As with any other part of learning how to use WordPerfect, the best experience is hands on.

The memo to the division heads (in figure 4–3) should still be on the screen. If it is not, press the Shift key and, while holding it down, press the F10 key. When asked, enter the name "divhead.mem", press the return key, and the memo will appear on your monitor screen. You will use this memo to practice making simple edits such as adding spaces and correcting misspellings.

WordPerfect Hint

If you run into trouble and the divhead.mem file is not on your screen, you can recall the contents of the corrected memo "divhead.mem" (which is also stored under the name divhead1.mem) by holding down the Shift key and pressing the F10 function key. Now type in the file name "divhead1.mem", and press the return key.

Later on in *Mastering WordPerfect,* you'll learn and practice more advanced editing techniques, such as moving text from one location in a document to another and making several changes throughout an entire document.

The Cursor Keys

As you learned earlier, the cursor is the short blinking horizontal line that shows your current location in the document you are working on. This is the most important function of the cursor. As you shall soon see, you can easily move from one part of a document to another. In some cases this might mean moving from one line to another, while in others, it might mean moving from one page to another.

To move the cursor, you will use one or more of a combination of **cursor control keys,** found on the right-hand side of the keyboard as shown in figure 5–1. Any one of these 10 keys (1, 2, 3, 4, 6, 7, 8, 9, +, and −), alone or in combination with other keys (such as pressing the home key twice and the 2 down arrow key), will move the cursor around the screen and the document.

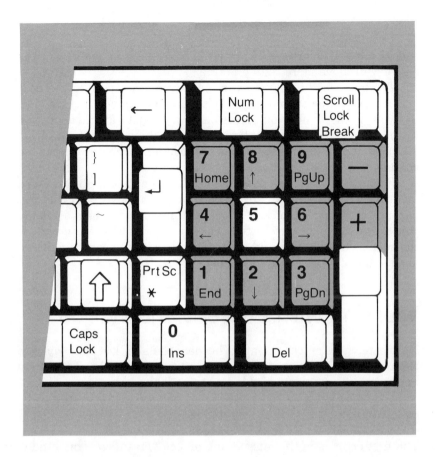

Figure 5–1   The Cursor Control Keys

Moving the cursor is the first step in any editing process since it takes you to the place where changes need to be made.

Moving Left and Right and Up and Down

You should still have the memo on the screen and can now practice using the cursor keys to move the cursor around the page and document.

First, there is a set of four **direction arrows** (the 8, 4, 6, and 2 keys) that control the movement of the cursor from line to line and from character to character along any one line.

The left arrow (on the number 4 key) and the right arrow (on the number 6 key) move the cursor one space to the left or right each time the key is depressed. If either of these keys is held down, the cursor will move more than one space.

The up arrow (on the number 8 key) and the down arrow (on the number 2 key) will move the cursor one line up or down each time the key is depressed. If either of these keys is held down, the cursor will move more than one line.

Try these four keys now and move from one space to the next and from one line to another. Don't worry where you end up placing your cursor since you can always move it to another location in the document. Notice that as you move the cursor, the position and line indicators in the lower right-hand corner of the screen change as well.

Regardless of where the cursor is in the memo after experimenting with these four keys, see if you can move it to the first letter A of the word August at the beginning of the memo. Before you begin working with letters and words, find the five errors in the memo. Circle them lightly in pencil in your book so you can keep track of what needs to be edited.

Working with Letters and Words

No matter how much editing is needed, the smallest unit you can work with is the letter. You'll begin editing at this level and then move on to larger parts of the document later.

Deleting Letters

The first error is in the misspelling of *Vcie- president*. This kind of error where letters are reversed is called a **reversal.**

To correct this misspelling, follow these steps.

1. Use the four cursor keys with arrows to move to the first letter in the word *Vcie-president*.

2. Place the cursor on (or under) the letter *c*.

3. Press the **delete key** (marked Del) twice. Both the *c* and the *i* should disappear.

4. Now, to make the corrections, simply type in the letters *i* and *c* in the correct order to spell *Vice*.

It's that simple to delete letters that you don't want and substitute ones that you do want.

Deleting Words

The second error is the appearance of the same word twice. In the first sentence, the phrase "will be be a. . ." appears. You want to delete one of the two appearances of the word *be*.

This can be done two ways. The first is to follow the same procedure as above. Place the cursor on the letter *b* and press the delete key twice. This erases the two letters of the word and leaves two spaces between *will* and *a*. Press the Del key once more to delete the extra space.

The second, and more efficient way, is to follow these steps:

1.   Place the cursor on the letter *b*.

2.   Press the Ctrl key, and while holding that key down, press the **Back Space** key located on in the upper right-hand corner of the keyboard.

The sequence of keystrokes looks like this: Ctrl→Backspace.

When this is done, the word the cursor is on (in this case the word *be*) will disappear. What's especially nice about this Word-Perfect feature is that the entire word, not just the letter, will be deleted.

WordPerfect Hint

Throughout Mastering WordPerfect *you will be asked to press several keys* in combination. *When one key needs to be held down while another is pressed, the instructions will look like this: key 1→key 2. Here key 1 is held down, while key 2 is pressed. Other times, you may be asked to press another key, after the first combination. This direction will look like this: key 1→key 2,1. Here, key 2 is pressed while key 1 is held down (as above), and then key 1 is released and the number 1 key is pressed.*

Inserting Letters

You have just deleted some letters and words from the memo in figure 4–2, and now it's time to insert letters in words that need them. The word "meting" in the first line of the memo needs another *e*. To add a letter (or letters), follow these steps.

1.   Move the cursor to where you want to add the letter. In this case it should be on the letter *e* in the word *meting*.

2.   To insert another *e*, simply type in the new letter.

You can see on your monitor screen how the word *meting* was changed to *meeting*.

Another insertion needed is a space between the words *your* and *recommendations* on line 3 of the first paragraph. A space is a character of sorts, only you can't see it!

Insert the space in the same way that you inserted the extra letter *e*. Move the cursor to the second *r* (yourrecommendations) and press the space bar once. WordPerfect makes space for letters and spaces because it is set up to automatically **insert** letters wherever they are typed. WordPerfect automatically moves everything else over to the right to make room for the new letters.

The Typeover and Insert Modes

Whenever you type in WordPerfect, there are two methods of entering text. One is the insert mode (which you should be in now), and the other is the **typeover mode.**

The insert mode automatically inserts characters between other characters wherever the cursor is placed. For example, if the cursor is on the letter *d* in the word *startd,* placing the cursor on the letter *d* and pressing the letter *e* will produce the correct spelling *started*.

On the other hand, the typeover mode would simply type the letter *e* over the letter *d* to produce the combination of letters *starte*. The typeover mode is selected by pressing the Ins or Insert key, to the left of the delete key. Try it now.

When you press it, you'll see the word *Typeover* appear on the lower left-hand corner of the screen. Press the Ins key again and you will see the message disappear as the mode returns to insert.

When to use which? It's probably best to work in the insert mode, unless you have a special application where you need to actually type over something. For example, if you have four different columns of names, such as

Bill	Susan	Jim	Jack
Mchael	William	Bob	John

inserting one letter in the first column (such as the *i* in *Michael)* moves the next word (William) over one space as shown below.

Bill	Susan	Jim	Jack
Michael	William	Bob	John

In this case a simple typeover of the letters "ichael" would have been more useful and saved you additional work.

Inserting Words

Inserting words is just like inserting letters. To insert a word, follow these steps.

1. Find the place where the new word is needed and move the cursor to that position.

2. Type the word.

In the memo shown in figure 4–2, the word *the* is missing from the next to last last line of the first paragraph. The phrase should read *of the month*. Insert the word *the* plus the necessary space.

You have just edited your first memo and are ready to move on to printing out a copy. Before you do, however, it's very important to save a copy of the changes you have made.

Saving Again

When you saved this memo the first time, you named it "divhead.mem", and WordPerfect remembers this. When you press the F10 function key to save all the changes you have made, WordPerfect gives you the same message as it did the first time, but it also includes the name of the file.

In this example, pressing the F10 key (do it now) will produce the following message in the bottom left corner of the screen:

Document to be Saved: A:\divhead.mem

Now, by pressing the return key, WordPerfect will begin saving the changes that you already made on the document under the same name.

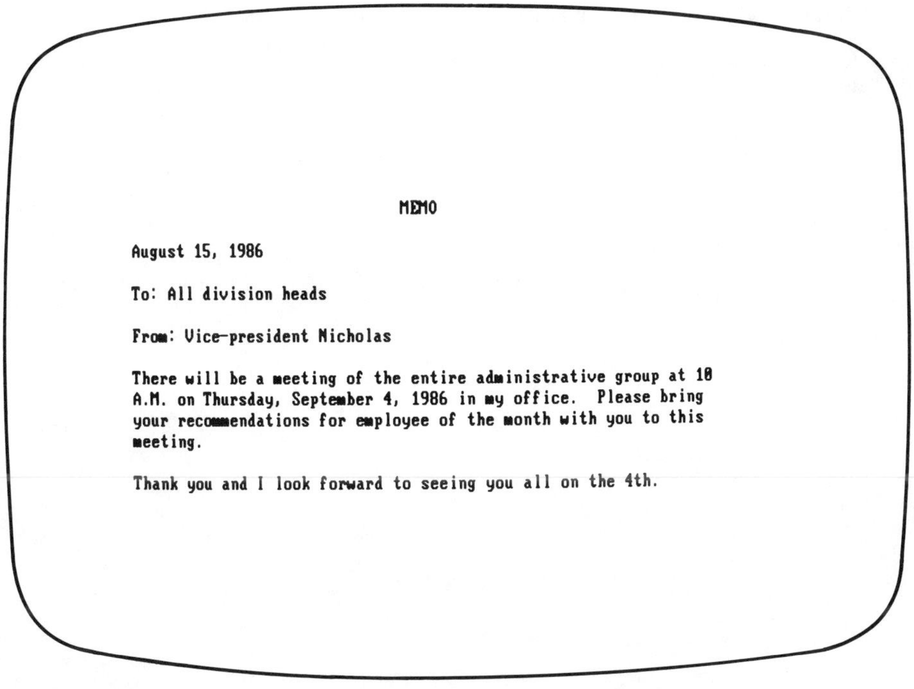

MEMO

August 15, 1986

To: All division heads

From: Vice-president Nicholas

There will be a meeting of the entire administrative group at 10 A.M. on Thursday, September 4, 1986 in my office. Please bring your recommendations for employee of the month with you to this meeting.

Thank you and I look forward to seeing you all on the 4th.

Figure 5–2   The Corrected Departmental Memo

But, as at many other times, WordPerfect wants to make sure that this is the name you want to use to save the file. So, instead of automatically saving it when you first push the F10 key, WordPerfect asks you whether you want to **replace** the existing file with this edited version of the document.

As you can see, WordPerfect does not automatically assume you want to replace the former version with the new version. It places an *N* after the question.

Replace a:\divhead.mem (Y/N)?N

To resave the file, enter the letter Y. The changes you made will be stored on the disk under the file name "divhead.mem".   The corrected memo is shown in figure 5–2. In later *Mastering Word-Perfect* lessons, you will recall this memo to help you learn about other WordPerfect features.

WordPerfect Hint

Remember, whatever changes you have made in a file when you are editing will replace the previous version of the text that you stored earlier.

You now have the memo corrected and saved and can move on to the WordPerfect feature that lets you actually see how much you have accomplished—printing a copy of your work.

LESSON 5 EXERCISES

1. After you have saved a document for the first time, each time thereafter you are actually *replacing* it. Under what conditions would you want to replace an existing file with another file name? How do you think this is done?

2. Here is a short paragraph that contains five different errors. Find each error and number it. Next to each number write out how you would correct that mistake, using which keys and what the corrected text would look like.

   > Last week, fiftenn people enrolled in thenew computer-
   > assisted instruction program. Each person person was
   > assigned a partner and both people sharred one computer.
   > All
   > in all, it was a very sucessful event. . .

3. Enter the following paragraph in your computer and correct words that are spelled correctly, but misused.

   > This is the first time that too of them had to bee with each
   > other. Both we're uncomfortable, butt wanted to continue
   > there work.

4. How do you use the backspace key to delete words? How do you use the delete key to delete a word?

5. Using the cursor keys, move the cursor to the 15th line and the 22nd column on the monitor screen. Why doesn't the document indicator change? How would you change the page (Pg) indicator using the down or up cursor keys?

6. What is the difference between the typeover and the insert modes? When would you use one rather than the other?

7. WordPerfect uses *combinations* of keys to begin certain commands. Write out what the following combinations require you to do, and what the combination of keys will do.

   (a) Shift→F10

   (b) Ctrl→Back Space

   (c) F1

LESSON 6
Printing Text

After this lesson you'll know

- What the print options menu looks like and what it does.
- How to print out a page or a complete file.
- How to preview a document.
- What a screen dump is and why it is important.

Important Terms

full text option	page option	print options menu
hard copy	preview	screen dump

Important Keys

Shift→F7	Shift→PrtSc	Shift→F7,6

A word processor would not be very useful if it could not print out or produce what is called a **hard copy** of your file. WordPerfect provides several ways to print out a document and also has options to help you customize the printing process.

_____

WordPerfect Hint

It is always easier to edit a document, be it a memo or a full-fledged report, from hard copy rather than on the monitor itself. Fatigue from eye strain makes it difficult to pick up and spot errors on the screen that might be very obvious on paper.

Printing the Memo

The first step is to make sure your printer is connected and working properly. Most printers come with programs that are built into the printer that allow you to check the printer's functions. The manual that came with your printer should have information about this. Also, be sure your printer is turned on. Once you are sure your printer is turned on and working, you need to do one more thing. If the memo from figure 5–2 is not still on your screen, recall it, using the Shift→F10 key combination and entering the name "divhead.mem".

Now press the combination of keys that brings up the Word-Perfect **print options menu** shown in figure 6–1.

To do this, depress the **Shift** key, and while that key is down, press the **F7** key like this: **Shift→F7.**

Printing the Complete Document

Of the six available choices on this printing menu, you'll learn about three. When the first option, marked **full text**, is selected (by pressing the 1 key), the entire contents of the file will be printed. This means that even the material not presently showing on the screen (but contained in the computer's RAM memory) will be printed, whether the file is 2 or 100 pages long. Option 1 is most frequently chosen, since the majority of the time you will want to print the entire document.

Printing a Page

When the second option, marked **Page**, is selected, *the page the cursor is on* is printed. This feature is handy when all you want to

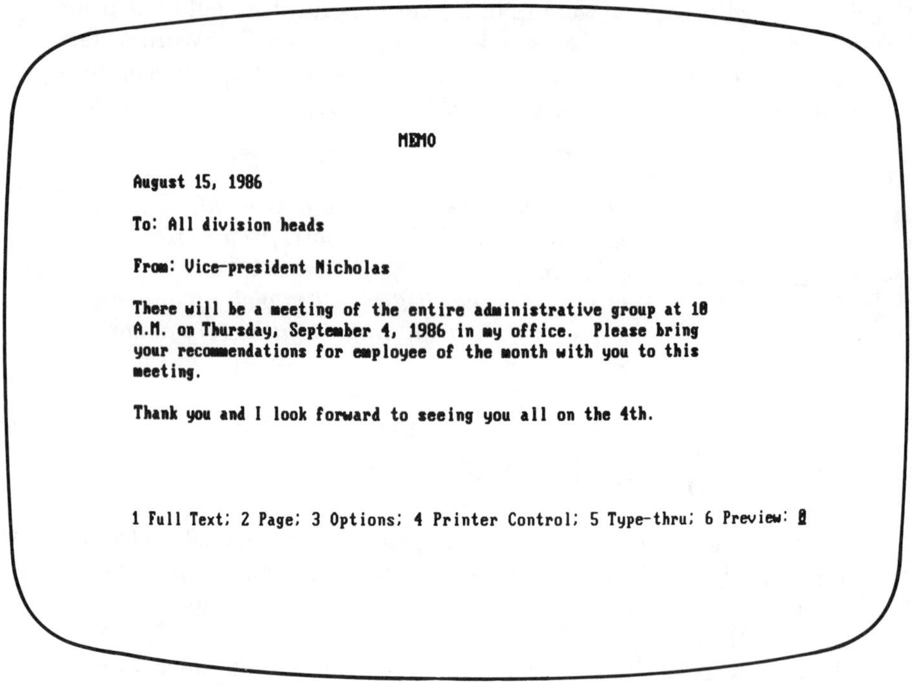

```
                              MEMO

          August 15, 1986

          To: All division heads

          From: Vice-president Nicholas

          There will be a meeting of the entire administrative group at 10
          A.M. on Thursday, September 4, 1986 in my office.  Please bring
          your recommendations for employee of the month with you to this
          meeting.

          Thank you and I look forward to seeing you all on the 4th.




          1 Full Text; 2 Page; 3 Options; 4 Printer Control; 5 Type-thru; 6 Preview: 0
```

Figure 6–1   Memo with Print Options Menu

print is one page of a longer document. If your document is only one page, then you can, of course, use either the print full document or print page features.

WordPerfect Hint

When in doubt about which print option to select, choose option 1, which will print out the entire file. In this way, if the file is longer than one page, you're safe. The page option is useful, but is probably most helpful when you need to print one page of a large document.

Select option 1 on the keyboard and the entire file with the memo should be printed. Do that now. Even though you are printing a relatively short file, keep in mind that you would do the same thing if you wanted to print the full copy of a 50-page report.

Previewing a Document

The last option to learn about in this lesson, **preview** (option 6), may be one of the most useful.

When you select this option, WordPerfect will allow you to see what your document will actually look like *when it is printed*. This will become especially valuable in part two of *Mastering Word-Perfect*, when you will be changing the appearance or format of your document and you may want to preview it before you print it.

With the memo shown in figure 5–2 on the screen, select the preview option by pressing the Shift→F7,6 combination. Word-Perfect gives you the choice of previewing by

1 Document; 2 Page

In this case, select 2 and wait. Shortly, you will see on your screen the way the memo will appear when it is printed.

WordPerfect Hint

*There is another way to print material, called a **screen dump,** which prints the exact contents of the monitor screen. This is not a WordPerfect option, but a function of your computer's design. Whatever you see on the screen will be printed, including the document, page, line, and position indicators. To dump a screen to the printer, press the Shift key and, while holding it down, press **the PrtSc** or print screen key like this: Shift→PrtSc. Your printer will then type out a copy of whatever image is on the screen.*

LESSON 6 EXERCISES

1. List five reasons why printing a document important.

2. What are some of the reasons why you might be unsuccessful when you are trying to print a document?

3. How often should you print out a copy of a document?

4. What is the difference between the full text and the page text options when you choose to print out a document?

5. Why would you choose to select the page option rather than the full text option when printing a document?

6. Identify and explain each of the print options that appears on the print options menu at the bottom of the monitor screen. What is each one used for? What are each one's advantages and disadvantages?

7. What does the instruction Shift→F7 require you to actually do? What would the instruction look like that directs you to press the Alt key, hold it down, press the F8 key, release both keys, and then press number 1 key?

8. When would the screen dump feature be useful?

9. Why would you want to use the screen dump feature instead of one of the other two print options discussed in this lesson?

LESSON 7
Clearing the Screen and Leaving WordPerfect

After this lesson you'll know

- How to clear your WordPerfect screen.
- How to leave the WordPerfect program.

Important Terms
clearing the screen   exiting

Important Keys
F7

You have just created, saved, edited, and printed a memo. This is the basic sequence of steps, shown in figure 1–1, for any kind of word processing job. When you are finished with these steps (and with the document you are working on), you may want to **clear the screen** and move on to another file.

Clearing the screen is just like erasing a chalkboard. The final result is a clean slate on which you can begin a new document. You might even want to leave WordPerfect altogether and turn off your computer system or move to a completely different software program.

When you want either to leave the WordPerfect file you are currently working on, or leave the WordPerfect program itself, WordPerfect makes sure that you don't accidentally lose any important files in the process. It's for this reason that, when you are sure you want to leave WordPerfect or clear the screen (and the computer's memory) to begin a new file, WordPerfect will first ask you if you want to save the file you just finished working on.

Clearing the WordPerfect Screen without Saving

To clear the WordPerfect screen, follow these steps. First, be sure you have the file named "divhead.mem" showing on your monitor screen.

1. Press the F7 key.

2. In response to the WordPerfect message at the bottom of your screen,

   Save Document (Y/N)? Y

   enter the letter N.

3. In response to the WordPerfect message at the bottom of your screen,

   Exit WordPerfect? (Y/N) N

   enter the letter N.

You should see a blank WordPerfect screen, identical to the opening screen shown in figure 3–1.

Saving the Document and Clearing the Screen

Perhaps you want to clear the screen *and* save the document. To save the document and clear the screen so you might recall another document, follow these steps. First, recall the file called "div-head.mem".

1. Press the F7 key.
2. In response to the WordPerfect message,

    Save Document (Y/N)? Y

    enter a Y, since you want to save the document.
        At this point, WordPerfect gives you the message

    Document to be Saved: A:divhead.mem

    giving you the chance to be sure that this is the document you want to save.
3. Press the return key to reveal the following message:

    Replace A:divhead.mem? (Y/N) N

    WordPerfect wants you to know that if you have made any changes *since the last save*, you will be replacing the *stored* or *saved* version of the memo, with the current active copy of the memo which is stored in RAM.
        Press the Y key, and the document will be saved.
4. The final key you need to press is the letter N, in response to the WordPerfect message

    Exit WordPerfect? (Y/N) N

Your document is saved and the WordPerfect screen is cleared.

Saving the Document and Exiting WordPerfect

If you want to save the document and **exit** WordPerfect, you would press the F7,Y key combination. Then, rather than responding N to the exit message, press the letter Y, and you will have saved the document and exited.

To Leave WordPerfect without Saving

To exit WordPerfect altogether without saving the document, follow these steps.

1. Follow the same two first steps as if you were clearing the screen and enter these keys: F7,N.

2. Instead of answering the Exit WordPerfect? question N, answer it Y. You should be returned to the system prompt, A>. If you try this, you will exit WordPerfect and will have to type **wp** to get back into WordPerfect.

The chart in figure 7–1 summarizes how you clear and/or exit WordPerfect.

You have just mastered the most basic features of the WordPerfect word processing system. What you learned in these seven lessons is enough for you to use WordPerfect for many of your word processing needs. Now it's time to move on to part two and more advanced and exciting WordPerfect features.

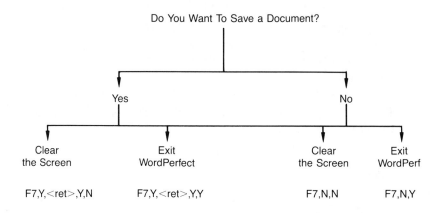

Figure 7–1   Clearing the WordPerfect Screen

LESSON 7 EXERCISES

1. When would you want (or need) to clear the WordPerfect screen?

2. There are four different options for clearing and/or exiting from the WordPerfect program. What are these options? Provide an example of when you would use each one.

3. Type in the following list of appointments and write down the sequence of keys that is necessary for you to clear the Word-Perfect screen without leaving WordPerfect.

> Ronda C.
> John P.
> Marvin F.
> Sandy P.
> Sheila N.
> Reva F.
> Audrey K.

4. Why should you always save a document one last time before leaving WordPerfect?

PART II

Advanced WordPerfect Techniques

If you are anything like thousands of other first time word processor users, you're probably thrilled at what you can now do with WordPerfect. Writing has never been easier and more fun! Even though you learned everything you need to enter, save, and print a document in the first part of *Mastering WordPerfect*, there are many other valuable features you have not yet been exposed to. These other features, such as global (throughout your entire document) searches, special formatting to change a document's appearance, and the ability to check for spelling errors will make you and WordPerfect even more successful as a word processing combination. Part two introduces you to these special features and more.

LESSON 8
Working with WordPerfect Files

After this lesson you'll know

- How to retrieve a file.
- How to "link" or "chain" files together.
- How to avoid "double documentitis".
- How much information is stored in a byte.
- How to change from the master disk to a work disk.
- What the WordPerfect list features menu is and why it is important.
- What the 10 options on the list features menu are.
- How to rename a file and why it is important.
- What a word pattern is and how to locate the files that contain a particular word pattern.

Important Terms

change directory	list files	word pattern
delete	rename	word search
directory	retrieve	work disk
insert a file	string	

Important Keys

F10	F5	Shift→F10

Up to now, you have created one document and saved it under the file name "divhead.mem". This was your first experience working with WordPerfect files that involved creating, editing, saving, and, finally, printing the contents of a file. Now it's time to move on and explore the other features that WordPerfect offers for working with files.

There are two ways of working with WordPerfect files. The first is by working directly from the keyboard, where you use one or a combination of keys to perform certain kinds of operations. For example, to save a file, you press the **F10** key.

The second way is through the use of the **list files** feature, which provides you with a menu of 10 different options you can perform on the file of your choice. The list files feature is especially helpful, since it allows you to perform many operations with only one keystroke. In this lesson, you will learn about working with files from both the keyboard, as well as the list files option.

Retrieving a File from the Keyboard

An important part of word processing is being able to **retrieve** or recall a file that has been saved. After a file is saved, you might want to return to that file and work on it again.

First, be sure your screen is clear. To retrieve a file with the keyboard, use the combination of Shift→F10 keys. When these are pressed, the message on the bottom of your screen is

Document to be Retrieved:

WordPerfect is asking you for the name of a document *that already exists* that you want to retrieve. WordPerfect will give you this message whether or not you are working on another document at that time.

If you try and retrieve a document that does not exist, WordPerfect will give you the this message: **ERROR: File Not Found** and ask you once again for the name of the file you want to retrieve. Type in the invalid file name "xxx" and press the return. WordPerfect gives you the error message **File Not Found** and asks you for another file name. Press the F1 key to return to a clear WordPerfect screen.

The WordPerfect training disk you received with this book already has some files on it that will be used for various exercises throughout *Mastering WordPerfect*. Your first exercise in retrieving a file involves recalling the two paragraph document shown in figure 8–1.

```
                            M E M O

        Date: October 18, 1986

        To: All sales representatives

        From: Richard Eisner, Sales Director

        I'm pleased to announce that our sales over the past six months
        have increased to a new level.  Much of the credit for this is
        due to your hard work and commitment.

        I look forward to the coming weeks and the announcement about our
        upcoming national sales meeting.




                                    Doc 1  Pg 1  Ln 1      Pos 10
```

Figure 8–1   Sales Memo

To recall this memo, follow these steps. First, be sure that your WordPerfect screen is blank.

1. Press the Shift and the F10 key. You will see the Document to be Retrieved message in the lower left hand corner of your screen.

2. Enter the file name "sales.mem"

3. Press the return key.

The memo from the sales director should be on the screen. That's all there is to recalling a single file.

WordPerfect Hint

Oops! A very common mistake occurs when one file is retrieved when another is already on the screen. You may end up with two (or even more) unrelated files following one another or "linked" together. This is useful if you want one file to follow another or want to place one file within another, as you'll see later. This is not very useful, however, if you only want one file on the

*screen at a time! This curious condition is
known as "double documentitis" and can be
cured only by completely erasing the screen
(F7→N,N), and then retrieving the document
you want to work with.*

Retrieving Multiple Files from the Keyboard

You just saw how simple it was to retrieve a single file in Word-
Perfect from the keyboard. You can also retrieve more than one
file the same way, but you need to make sure you know what you
need and what you want to do.

You should still have the "sales.mem" on your WordPerfect
screen, as shown in figure 8–1. Perhaps the sales director wants to
enter additional information from another file called "sales. dat"
(shown in figure 8–2) into this sales memo.

One way the sales director could combine the two would be to
type the sales information directly into the "sales.mem" file. An-

Sales from 4/1/86 through 18/1/86

Region	Sales	Percent Increase*
1	26.2	.8
2	31.5	7.4
3	33.7	.7
4	22.7	3.1
5	18.9	5.5

*Increase over the last six months

Figure 8–2   Sales Data Information

other more efficient way would be to **insert the file** (sales.dat) directly into the sales memo. Follow these steps to enter the "sales.dat" information into the original sales memo file.

1. Be sure that the "sales.mem" file is on your screen. If not, recall it as you did earlier in this lesson.

2. Move the cursor to the first line after the first paragraph, which ends with the word *commitment*, and then press the return key to move the cursor down one more line.

3. Press the Shift and the F10 key. You will see the Document to be Retrieved message appear at the bottom of the screen.

4. Now enter the file name "sales.dat" (notice that this is a completely new file).

5. Press the return key.

Your screen should look exactly like the screen shown in figure 8–3, which shows a combination of both files.

There are several ways to use WordPerfect's retrieve files feature. For example, what if you were writing a report with many

```
                        M E M O

     Date: October 10, 1986

     To: All sales representatives

     From: Richard Eisner, Sales Director

     I'm pleased to announce that our sales over the past six months
     have increased to a new level. Much of the credit for this is
     due to your hard work and commitment.

                  Sales from 4/1/86 through 10/1/86


         Region        Sales        Percent Increase*
           1           26.2              .8
           2           31.5             7.4
           3           33.7              .7
           4           22.7             3.1
           5           18.9             5.5

     *Increase over the last six months

     I look forward to the coming weeks and the announcement about our
     upcoming national sales meeting.

                              Doc 1  Pg 1  Ln 47      Pos 10
```

Figure 8–3   Sales Memo and Sales Data Information Combined

different sections? You don't want to have one tremendous file, since large files take a long time to save. It is also risky if that one large file should be damaged or accidentally erased.

Instead, you store your files as "sec1", "sec2", etc. When the time comes to print out the entire report, you first retrieve the file "sec1", go to the end of that file (use the home, cursor down, cursor down key combination), and then retrieve the file named "sec2", and so on. Soon you have all 20 sections *linked* together into one document.

The only thing you need to be careful of is that the group of linked files has the same name as the first file you retrieved. To avoid any problems, make a copy of the first file under the name you want to use for the entire set of linked files, then begin adding or linking the files together.

The List Files Feature

There is another way to manage WordPerfect files that allows you to complete the majority of necessary operations with only one keystroke. This is the list files feature of WordPerfect, activated by pressing the F5 key.

Pressing this key at any time, regardless whether you have an active file or a blank screen in front of you, will provide a list of all the files in a particular **directory**, plus other important information. A directory is a list of files on a particular disk. Before you actually begin working with the list files feature, clear the WordPerfect screen.

To use the list files feature, follow these steps.

1. Press the F5 key.

2. You should see a message on the bottom of your screen, shown in figure 8–4:

    Dir A:*.* (Type = to change to default directory)

    This WordPerfect message is telling you that the directory that will be listed contains all the files (*.*) in directory A (which is the same as the files listed on the disk in disk drive A).

3. Once you see the above message, press the return key and you should shortly see the screen shown in figure 8-5.

    This screen reveals general information about directory A, the list of files on the disk in drive A, specific information about each file, and a set of ten different options, such as deleting or printing a file, from which you can choose for any one file. For example, you

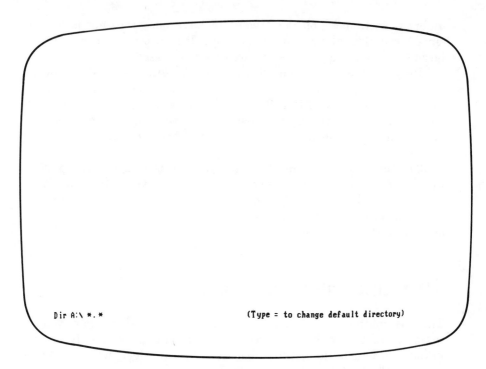

Dir A:\ *.*   (Type = to change default directory)

Figure 8–4   List Files Menu Message

might recognize the file titled "divhead.mem" as the file you
worked with earlier and the "sales.mem" as two files you've
worked with before.

What follows is a more extensive discussion of the list files feature of WordPerfect found on the menu shown in figure 8–5.

The List Files Screen

The most visible feature in figure 8–5 is the list of all the files on
the directory. You can also see the date and time that the list files
feature was requested, the name of the directory, the size of the
document that is currently being worked on, and how much space
is free on the disk for additional entries.

Look at the actual list of files and you can see how each file is
listed (with its extension), the amount of space that it takes up,
and the date and time that it was created. These last two features
are automatically entered based on the information that you provided when you booted up or started your system. For example, the
file "lew.ltr" (a letter to lew) was created on 12/2/86 at 9:29.

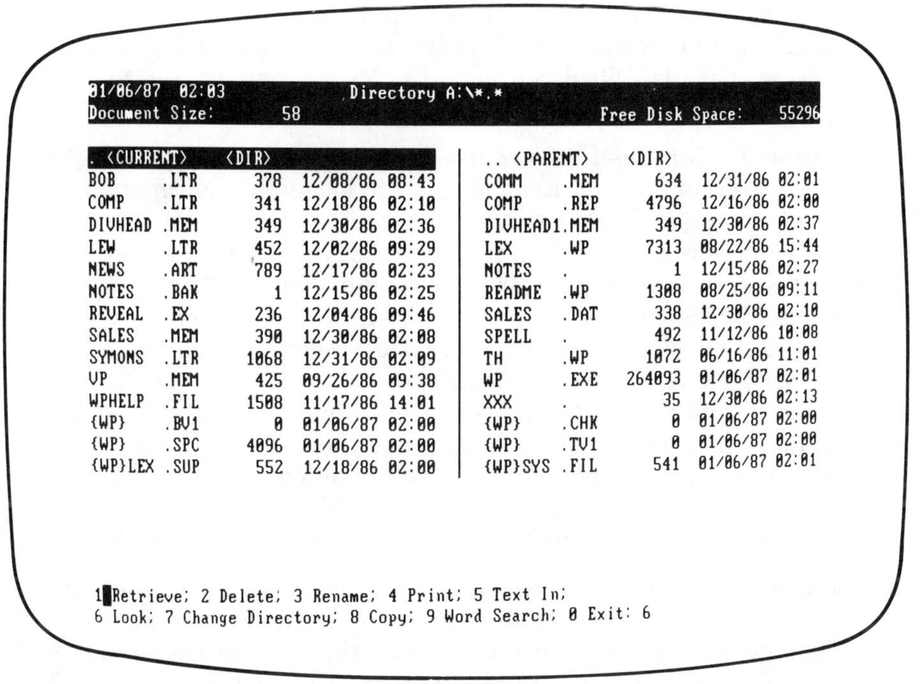

```
01/06/87  02:03          Directory A:\*.*
Document Size:       58                       Free Disk Space:     55296

. <CURRENT>     <DIR>               .. <PARENT>     <DIR>
BOB      .LTR      378  12/08/86 08:43  COMM     .MEM      634  12/31/86 02:01
COMP     .LTR      341  12/18/86 02:10  COMP     .REP     4796  12/16/86 02:00
DIVHEAD  .MEM      349  12/30/86 02:36  DIVHEAD1.MEM      349  12/30/86 02:37
LEW      .LTR      452  12/02/86 09:29  LEX      .WP      7313  08/22/86 15:44
NEWS     .ART      789  12/17/86 02:23  NOTES    .           1  12/15/86 02:27
NOTES    .BAK        1  12/15/86 02:25  README   .WP      1308  08/25/86 09:11
REVEAL   .EX       236  12/04/86 09:46  SALES    .DAT      338  12/30/86 02:10
SALES    .MEM      390  12/30/86 02:00  SPELL    .           492  11/12/86 10:08
SYMONS   .LTR     1068  12/31/86 02:09  TH       .WP      1072  06/16/86 11:01
VP       .MEM      425  09/26/86 09:38  WP       .EXE   264093  01/06/87 02:01
WPHELP   .FIL     1508  11/17/86 14:01  XXX      .          35  12/30/86 02:13
{WP}     .BV1        0  01/06/87 02:00  {WP}     .CHK        0  01/06/87 02:00
{WP}     .SPC     4096  01/06/87 02:00  {WP}     .TV1        0  01/06/87 02:00
{WP}LEX  .SUP      552  12/18/86 02:00  {WP}SYS  .FIL      541  01/06/87 02:01


1 Retrieve; 2 Delete; 3 Rename; 4 Print; 5 Text In;
6 Look; 7 Change Directory; 8 Copy; 9 Word Search; 0 Exit: 6
```

Figure 8–5   List Files Menu Screen

The List Files Options

There are 10 different options you can select from the list files option. These are all shown on the bottom of figure 8–5.

To select any one of the 10 options, you need to first move to the name of the file you want using the cursor keys. Then, press the number of the option you want to perform.

Try moving up and down the list of files using the cursor keys. When you move the cursor key to a particular place, you can see how the selected file is shown in *reverse video*. As you can see, you can move up or down, or left or right to choose a file.

Option 1 - Retrieve This option allows you to **retrieve** a file from the list files feature and it places you in that file. Move the cursor to the "sales.mem" file and then press the 1 key. As you should see on your screen, that file is immediately recalled and you are ready to work.

Now clear the screen (F7→N,N) and return to the list files options (F5,<ret>).

Option 2 - Delete This option allows you to **delete** or erase a file from the disk. To delete a file, press the 2 key *after* the file has been selected. For example, move the cursor to the file marked "XXX", and press the 2 key. WordPerfect will ask you if you want to erase that file. When you press the Y key, you will see the file disappear from the list files menu.

Option 3 - Rename In the course of working with files, you might need to **rename** a file. Renaming a file keeps the information in the file intact, but only changes its name.

When you select 3, WordPerfect asks you (in the bottom left hand corner of the screen) for the **new name** of the file. When this information is entered, and when the return key is pressed, you will see the new name of the file replace the existing name.

Why rename a file? You might do this when you are "house-cleaning" and find that two files have similar names and need different names. You will want to change them to reflect their contents. For example, you might have a file called "Jim.ltr" and need to write a letter to another Jim. You could then change the first file from "Jim.ltr" to "JimG.ltr" and name the new file "JimF.ltr".

Option 4 - Print If you should want to print a copy of a file directly from the list files option, simply select the file and press the 4 key. Remember to be sure that your printer is turned on and is on line. Move the cursor to highlight the "divhead.mem" file and print it out.

Option 5 - Text In This is a special WordPerfect feature that allows you to change a WordPerfect file to a DOS file or change a DOS file to a WordPerfect file. This option is usually reserved for technical applications.

Option 6 - Look What a nice feature this is! There will be times when you have many different files on a disk and you are not sure what is contained in one or another file. The Look option allows you to view the contents of a file.

For example, move the cursor to the "sales.mem" file and press the 6 key. Your screen should show you the contents of that file, as shown in figure 8–1, along with additional information.

On the top of the screen you can see the file name (on drive A), and the size of the file in bytes or pieces of information. Then you can see the contents of the actual file and a message on the bottom of the screen telling you that the file is not in WordPerfect format, meaning that you could not make any changes on the file at this point.

If you want to edit the file, you need to return to the list files features and retrieve the file (option 1) to work on it. Press any key at this point to return to the list files menu.

You might also notice that at the bottom of the list files menu screen, the number 6 is listed last. This is the default, and anytime you press the Enter key, WordPerfect will automatically give you a "look" at whatever file you have selected.

Option 7 - Change Directory You may want to **change the directory** or the disk that you are working on. You can do this by using this List Files option. This will be discussed in greater detail in the next section of this lesson, Changing Work Disks.

Option 8 - Copy The copy option allows you to make a copy of a file on to another disk, or even to make a copy of a file on to the same disk under another name. For example, what if you wanted to make a copy of the "sales.dat" file and store it on the same disk? First, move the cursor bar over the file name "sales.dat" on the file list. Then, pressing the 8 key produces the following message:

Copy This File To:

WordPerfect wants you to do one of two things: either copy this file onto another disk using the same or a different name, or make a copy of this file on the same disk the file is already on using a different file name.

One reason you might want to copy a file onto another disk is for safekeeping. That way you would have two copies of the same file on different disks so that if anything should happen to one disk, you have the other as a backup.

But why would you want to make a copy of the same file on the same disk? Well, you might want to make a copy of a file and then change it slightly. For example, you could make a copy of the "sales.dat" file, then add a note to an interested employee, or even change the heading or the information itself if necessary.

If you want to copy a file onto a disk where it already occurs, WordPerfect requires that a different name be used for the new file. For example, to make a copy of the file "sales.dat", type in the following at the "Copy This File Message": a:\sales2.dat. This 2 added to the name distinguishes it from the file named "sales.dat", containing the same information. The new file will not appear immediately on the list of files, even though it has been created. The next time you list files, it will appear as part of the list.

Option 9 - Word Search This provides you with a quick and easy way to find out in what files a certain character, word, or phrase appears. This is very useful if you should forget in what file something occurs and you need to find it quickly.

To use this option, you need not worry about selecting a file to search, since WordPerfect will search *all* the files in a directory and look for the **word pattern** you designate.

When you press the 9 key, WordPerfect asks you for a word

pattern as shown in figure 8–6. Enter the word "region" since you want to find information on regional sales. Press the return key. WordPerfect will then search through each file and list the files where the word region is used. This process takes time, so be patient. WordPerfect will eventually identify the file "sales.dat", shown in figure 8–7, as the files that contain the word. You can ask WordPerfect to search for a **string** of up to 20 characters. A string is a set of characters, including spaces.

WordPerfect Hint

To use the Word Search option efficiently, try to give WordPerfect as much information as you can. For example, if you are looking for the words the sales meeting, *search for all three words, and not just* the *(of which there are many occurrences). WordPerfect will be able to work faster and will give you the most accurate return if you provide as much information as possible.*

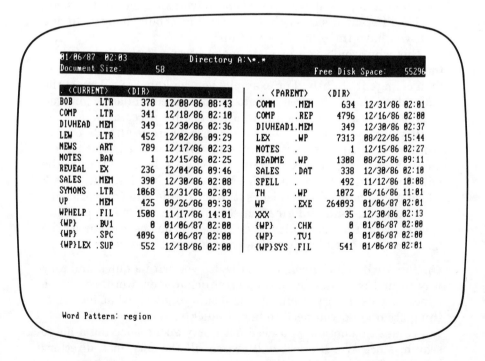

01/06/87 02:03			Directory A:*.*			
Document Size:		58			Free Disk Space:	55296
. <CURRENT>	<DIR>			.. <PARENT>	<DIR>	
BOB .LTR	378	12/08/86 08:43		COMM .MEM	634	12/31/86 02:01
COMP .LTR	341	12/18/86 02:10		COMP .REP	4796	12/16/86 02:00
DIVHEAD .MEM	349	12/30/86 02:36		DIVHEAD1.MEM	349	12/30/86 02:37
LEW .LTR	452	12/02/86 09:29		LEX .WP	7313	08/22/86 15:44
NEWS .ART	789	12/17/86 02:23		NOTES .	1	12/15/86 02:27
NOTES .BAK	1	12/15/86 02:25		README .WP	1308	08/25/86 09:11
REVEAL .EX	236	12/04/86 09:46		SALES .DAT	338	12/30/86 02:10
SALES .MEM	390	12/30/86 02:08		SPELL .	492	11/12/86 10:08
SYMONS .LTR	1068	12/31/86 02:09		TH .WP	1072	06/16/86 11:01
UP .MEM	425	09/26/86 09:38		WP .EXE	264093	01/06/87 02:01
WPHELP .FIL	1508	11/17/86 14:01		XXX .	35	12/30/86 02:13
{WP} .BV1	0	01/06/87 02:00		{WP} .CHK	0	01/06/87 02:00
{WP} .SPC	4096	01/06/87 02:00		{WP} .TV1	0	01/06/87 02:00
{WP}LEX .SUP	552	12/18/86 02:00		{WP}SYS .FIL	541	01/06/87 02:01

Word Pattern: region

Figure 8–6   Search for Word Pattern "region"

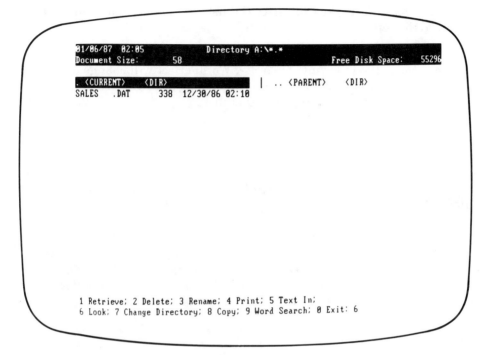

```
01/06/87  02:05              Directory A:\*.*
Document Size:        58                      Free Disk Space:    55296

. <CURRENT>   <DIR>              |  .. <PARENT>   <DIR>
SALES   .DAT      338  12/30/86 02:10




















 1 Retrieve; 2 Delete; 3 Rename; 4 Print; 5 Text In;
 6 Look; 7 Change Directory; 8 Copy; 9 Word Search; 0 Exit: 6
```

Figure 8–7   Files Containing Word Pattern "region"

Changing Work Disks (or Changing Directories)

Up to this point, you have been working on disk drive A, which contained your master WordPerfect disk. In other words, you have been using your WordPerfect disk as a **work disk**, which is the place where you are storing your newly created files.

As you probably know, files take up space, and your Word-Perfect disk is getting fuller as more files are created. So, it's time to learn how to change from working on the disk in drive A to the blank disk that you formatted in lesson 2 and labeled as work disk 1.

To begin creating, storing, and working with files on another disk, follow these simple steps. Be sure to exit from the list files option by pressing the **0** key.

1. Place the formatted disk in drive B (see figure 2–1 if you don't know drive A from drive B).

2. Press the F5 key to select the list files option and then press the return key.

3. Select the change directory option by pressing the 7 key.

4. Enter the following: b: <ret>. WordPerfect will change over to the B drive and all operations including saving, retrieving, and so forth will take place on that disk.

WordPerfect Hint

You might want to create separate work disks, depending upon your needs. For example, one work disk might be used only for papers and reports, while another would be used for letters. Or, there could be separate work disks for different people in the household or the department in which you work. This way, people can keep their work separate from others'. This usually helps keep things organized and helps manage work assignments.

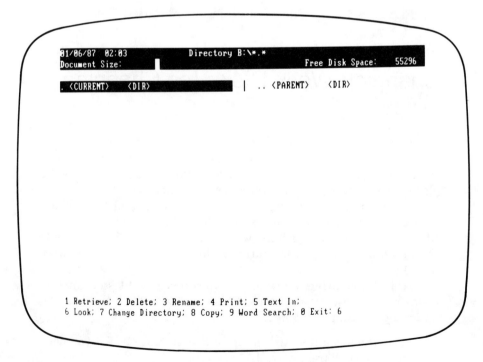

Figure 8–8   List Files Menu for a New Disk

WordPerfect will also list all the files that are contained on the disk in drive B. Since this is a newly formatted disk, there should be no files listed, as shown in figure 8–8. Since all the WordPerfect training files are on disk A (the master disk), change the directory back to disk A using option 7.

Repeating a List Files Command

There may be an occasion when you want to perform the same operation on more than one file. For example, what if you wanted to print out five files, without having to select and press the 4 key five separate times? You can do this by simply selecting a file and then marking it with an *asterisk* (*). For example, if you wanted to print the files named "CH1", "CH2", and "CH3", you could select and star each one and then press the 4 key.

WordPerfect will ask you if you want to print all files, and you respond by pressing Y. You can do this to delete, print, or copy a group of files. For example, it is a good idea at the end of each work day to copy all of the files you worked with that day over to another floppy disk as a backup.

What if you mistakenly starred an item and want to remove the asterisk? Just use the cursor keys to go back and click the asterisk key again on the same file. The asterisk will be removed. Using the WordPerfect feature that allows you to repeat the copy command is very helpful and saves a good deal of time.

Leaving the List Files Feature

To exit from the list files feature and return to the WordPerfect operating screen, press the 0 option, which is Exit.

LESSON 8 EXERCISES

1. How does "double documentitis" happen and what can you do to avoid it?

2. List the specific commands that you would need to
    a) rename a file from "train.sch" to "train1.sch".
    b) copy file "abc" from disk B to disk A.
    c) find the string "home address"
    d) retrieve the file "c1c2.ltr".

3. What is the Look feature of the list files menu and why is it a valuable tool? How would you use it during your word processing activities?

4. What would the sequence of steps be to make an exact copy of a file located on disk A?

5. Write out the sequence of steps to erase the files "link1" and "link2" from your disk.

6. Here are some words and phrases that are contained in a set of files. For each one, comment on why or why not it is a good set to use with the word search option on the list files menu.
    a) the
    b) about the same as he did
    c) on the
    d) Rachel Marston

7. You are working on a book that is 10 chapters long and have created a separate file for each chapter named "ch1.bk", "ch2.bk", etc. List the set of steps that you would take to retrieve or link all of these chapters together.

8. Among the files on your training disk are "link1" and "link2". Each file has one name and address.
    a) Retrieve "link1", rename it "address"
    b) Retrieve "link2"
    c) Save the newly created file that now has two names and addresses under its new name.

9. Provide three examples in which the word search feature of WordPerfect would be helpful.

10. What is the difference between a work and a data disk? Why don't you store all your data on your work disk?

LESSON 9
Advanced Editing Techniques: Moving Around

After this lesson you'll know

- How to move word by word through a line of text.
- How to move the cursor from one part of a line to another part of the same line.
- How to move through a document screen by screen (24 lines at a time).
- How to move through a document page by page (54 lines at a time).
- How to move from the beginning to the end of a document or from the end to the beginning of a document.

Important Terms

block	page cursor	screen cursor
document cursor	movement	movement
movement	screen down	word cursor movement
line cursor movement	screen up	

Important Keys

− key	Home/Home/Down	Home/Right cursor
+ key	cursor arrow	arrow
Ctrl/left cursor arrow	Home/Home/Up	Home/Up cursor arrow
Ctrl/right cursor arrow	cursor arrow	PgDn
Home/Down cursor	Home/Left cursor	PgUp
arrow	arrow	Shift/F10

In lesson 5, you learned how to use the cursor keys to move from one place to another on a WordPerfect page and to delete and insert letters and lines. Those skills are fundamental to editing any document. Now it's time to go beyond those basics and begin learning more advanced editing techniques such as deleting large parts of a document or using *blocks*, sections of text that you define and perform some operation on.

Retrieving A Practice File

You have already learned an important part of working on any document—being able to store it. Storing a file (and finding it again!) is critical. Yet, as important as this WordPerfect feature is, recalling or retrieving a file is just as critical.

As you learned in lesson 8, you retrieve a file by asking WordPerfect to find a file that is on your master or work disk and "load" it into your computer's active memory.

```
                    Software for Children
        Here are some of the really outstanding children's and
    family software that I have come across in the last few months
    during my marketing activities.  We should seriously consider
    making them part of regular offerings to our customers. Most of
    them are reasonably priced, readily available, and may be
    successful items, especially during the holiday sales period.


        Auto Builder gives that budding automotive engineer in the
    family, a chance to design, construct, modify and even test his


    ^^^^^^^^^^^^^^^^^^^^^^^^^^^^^^^^^^^^^^^^^^^^^^^^^^^^^^^^^^^^^^^^^


        Writer Rabbit is an easy and efficient way to personalize a
    set of writing exercises for 5 to 7 year olds.  The parent,
    teacher, or student can also get help at any time by simply
    pressing the "?" (what else!) key.
        Math Fun (for 3-5 year olds) is the most entertaining math
    program that I have seen for this age group.  The animation
    sequences find children invited to a party and elephants moving
    across the screen "trunk-in-tail", just like the real thing.




                              Doc 1  Pg 1  Ln 48     Pos 10
```

Figure 9–1   Computer Report Practice File

Don't forget that whenever you retrieve a file, it will be "added on" to what's already on your screen, possibly causing confusion as to what's what. Always clear your screen before you retrieve a new file unless you want to link or join files.

In this lesson, you will practice editing techniques such as moving from one page to another. On your master WordPerfect disk there is already a two-page document for you to use. The document is a newspaper review of some children's computer programs. The beginning and the end of the report are shown in figure 9–1.

In order to practice page and document cursor movements, you need to recall the document shown in figure 9–1 named "comp.rep".

Use the Shift→F10 key combination, type in the file name, "comp.rep," and press the return key. You should see a copy of the report on your monitor screen. This is the practice file that you will work with for this lesson.

More Cursor Movements

You already know how to use the cursor keys to move from one space to another and from line to line. The four arrow keys on the numeric keypad (see figure 5–1) can be used to move the cursor one space or one line at a time.

Now it's time to use the WordPerfect tools that allow you to move much larger "distances," such as from word to word, to the beginning or end of a line, to the end or beginning of an entire document, or any place you want, all with *very few* keystrokes.

Remember, all cursor movements for lines, screens, pages, and documents use the keys on the numeric keypad located on the right hand side of your keyboard and highlighted in figure 5–1.

Word Cursor Movements

You already know that the simplest cursor movements are from one letter to another, and you practiced these in an earlier *Mastering WordPerfect* lesson. The next step up from these simple movements is moving across a line (or through a document) **word by word.** Here you use the Ctrl and the → or the ← keys to move from one word to the next.

With the "comp.rep" file on the screen, move the cursor to the fifth line of text (use the line indicator), beginning with *making them part of a ......*

To move one word to the right, hold down the Ctrl key and press the → (right cursor) arrow once. Do this once to move to the beginning of the word *them*.

To move one word to the left, hold down the Ctrl key and press the ← (left cursor) arrow once. Do this once to move back to the beginning of the line. The cursor should now be on the letter *m* of the word *making*.

What happens if you continue to move the cursor word by word? When it gets to the end of the line, it will simply move on to the next line. But since you can move to that one line through the use of the down arrow cursor key, why not just do that rather than move word by word? In any WordPerfect cursor movement, try and use the editing technique that is the most efficient.

Line Cursor Movements

The simplest cursor movement, besides moving only one space or word at a time, is from one end of a line to the other end. For this, use the Home, → or Home, ← keystroke combinations.

To practice moving from one end of a line to another, do the following:

1. Use the four cursor keys to move to the beginning of the first line of the document, beginning with *Here are some of the really* . . . . The cursor should be blinking under the letter *H*.

2. Press the Home key and then the right cursor arrow key (→) one right after the other. Don't hold the home key down while you press the cursor arrow key. The cursor should move from the left end of the line to the right end of the line.

If you want to move from the right end of the line to the left end, press the Home key and the left cursor arrow key (←), one right after the other. The cursor should move from the right end of the line to the left end of the line.

Practice moving from one end of a line to the other on several different lines until you feel comfortable moving from one side of the document to the other.

Now move up to the first line in the review, "Software for Children," and use the Home and Cursor arrows to move the cursor back and forth across the page. Notice that when you move the cursor to the right, it only goes as far as one space past the last character on the line. This is because you are going to the end of the line and not to the end of the screen.

Screen Cursor Movements

Another simple cursor movement is to move the cursor from one part of the monitor screen to another. Using the plus (+) key or minus (−) key, you can move to the top or the bottom of your monitor *screen*. Remember, when you move from the top to the bottom or from the bottom to the top of the screen, you are only moving through the part of the document that is currently visible on the monitor itself.

Your screen should still contain the software review file and the cursor should be at the top left. Use the cursor arrow keys to get to that position if the cursor is not there now.

To move to the bottom left-hand corner of the screen, press the plus key (+) *on the numeric key pad*. When you do this, the cursor should move to the last line of the screen. Remember, the **screen up** key is located on the numeric keypad. If you press the plus key on the top line of keys, you will get the "plus" character and the cursor will not move at all. To move back to the first line of the screen, move the minus key (−) *on the numeric keypad*. When you do this, the screen will appear to move down.

Do both of these a few times to get some idea of how fast the movement is and where the cursor ends up after the move.

What happens when you are on the last line of the screen and press the + (**screen down**) key again? You'll automatically go to the bottom of what would be the next monitor screen. Unless directed otherwise, WordPerfect shows 24 single spaced lines on a monitor screen. Every time you press the screen down and screen up keys, you will move 24 lines.

WordPerfect Hint

Some people only like to use the nine keys on the numeric pad and nothing else to move the cursor. You can accomplish the same thing as + and − by using the Home and the up cursor arrow to move to the top of the screen and the Home and the down cursor arrow to move to the bottom.

Page Cursor Movements

You can not only move from one part of a line or a screen to another, but also from one page in a document to another. You can move by pages using the PgUp and PgDn keys that are located on the numeric keypad on the 9 and the 3 keys. When you use the PgDn command, you automatically move to the top of the next *page* (not the next screen).

WordPerfect is preset to have 54 lines of text on any page, but to show only 24 of those lines (and only 12 if the page is double-spaced) on the screen. Each time you move the cursor using the PgUp and PgDn keys, you move 54 lines. Remember, when you move this many lines, and your screen can show only 24, you will not see some information (the last 30 lines of the screen) when you page through. The information is, of course, still there, but since you are skipping material on a page, you will not see it.

For example, if you are at the first line of the report beginning with *Here are some. . . .*, and you press the PgDn key, you will automatically be placed on the first line of the next page, which begins with *more fun. . . .*

If you look at the page, line, and document indicators at the lower right hand corner of the screen, you will notice that you are on page 2, line 1, position 10.

To move to the top of the previous page, use the PgUp key. To move to the beginning of the following page, use the PgDn key. If you want to move more than one page, just press the key more than once. You can page up or down through an entire document.

Document Cursor Movements

WordPerfect has two other sets of keystrokes that can move you to the beginning or end of a document very quickly.

To move to the end of a document, the following sequence of keys is pressed (with none being held down): Home,Home,down cursor arrow

To practice this, move your cursor to the top of the first page of the computer report. Now press this sequence of keys and see how what shows on the screen is the last page of the report, with the cursor located at the end of the last line in the document, which reads *. . . .like the real thing,* as shown in figure 9–1.

You may notice that when you move through the entire document, WordPerfect gives you a message in the lower left hand corner that reads

Repositioning

To move to the beginning or top of a document, press the following sequence of keys: Home,Home,up cursor arrow. Try this now and see both the repositioning message and how the first 24 lines of the first page show on your screen.

By this time, you should have a good idea how to move the cursor around by space, by line, by screen, by page, and by document by pressing one of the eight cursor keys (all the number keys except the number 5) or some combination. Be sure to consult the quick reference section in the WordPerfect Extras section of this book if you should have any question about what set of keyboard commands to use. If you practice your WordPerfect, you will find that using these commands becomes almost second nature.

A Summary of What to Use When

You'll find that the more you use WordPerfect the faster you will get at using the cursor movement combinations to edit your documents. One way to remember which method to use is to think of all the choices ranging from small changes to big ones.

Make the smallest changes with the right and left cursor arrows to move from letter to letter. Use the Ctrl and the right and left cursor arrows to move words. The up and down cursor arrows move from line to line. The screen cursor movement keys (+) and (−) move you 24 lines. Next are the PgUp and PgDn keys, which move you an entire page, or 54 lines. Finally, use the double strike of the home key with the up or down cursor arrows to move to the beginning or the end of a document.

LESSON 9 EXERCISES

Clear your WordPerfect screen, and recall the file "comp.rep" just as you did earlier in the lesson.

1. Now that you have it on your screen, what is the fastest way to move to the top of page 2?

2. What is the best way to move from the beginning of the third line of actual text (*family software. . .*) to the end of that line? How would you return to the beginning of that line?

3. How many times would you need to use the PgDn key to move from the beginning to the end of a 15-page document?

Clear your WordPerfect screen once again. Now retrieve the document "divhead.mem".

4. How would you move to the bottom right hand corner of the page with only one keystroke?

5. When would you want to use the + or − keys to move only one screen rather than an entire page?

6. When you move from the beginning of a document to the end, how do you know that the move is taking place and what should you look at to know that the move is finished?

LESSON 10
Deleting and Moving Text

After this lesson you'll know

- How to delete entire lines, pages, and parts of a WordPerfect document.

- How to undelete or reverse deleting text you may have mistakenly started to delete.

- How to create and use blocks to move, delete, and print entire sections of documents.

- How WordPerfect can automatically create blocks of sentences and paragraphs.

Important Terms

append block	cut block	restore
copy block	highlight	undelete
	move	

Important Keys

Alt→F4	Ctrl→F4	Ctrl→PgDn
Ctrl→End		

Deleting Lines and Pages

Editing involves moving around lines, pages, and a document, but it also involves deleting text when necessary. Although you might not plan on it, you may sometimes need to delete lines or even entire pages from your document. WordPerfect offers several quick and easy ways to delete.

WordPerfect Hint

Remember, when you delete anything from a document that is active in your computer and showing on your monitor screen, the actual copy of the file on your floppy disk is not changed. It is only when you save the document after making changes (and WordPerfect asks you "Replace. . ."), that the actual file itself is changed. You can do whatever you want to text on the screen (or in your computer's memory), but nothing is changed on the actual file until you use the F10 key to save. One thing this means is that you can always go back to the original file (on the floppy disk) if necessary, as long as you did not already save your changes.

Deleting a Line

To delete an entire line or part of a line, follow these steps.

1. Place the cursor at the point on the line where you want to begin deleting.

2. Press the Ctrl key, and, while holding it down, press the End key (on the numeric keypad). This will automatically erase everything *to the right of the cursor*. If you want to erase an entire line, then you must place the cursor on the first letter of the first word on that line and press the key combination Ctrl→End.

For some hands-on practice deleting, clear your WordPerfect screen and retrieve the file named "lew.ltr." shown in figure 10–1.

Using the down cursor arrow key, move the cursor to the beginning of the last line of the letter

P.S. Please find . . .

The post script is no longer needed. Now use the Ctrl→End key

December 2, 1986

Lew Margolin
Consumer's Affairs
1822 West 5th Street
Williams, Michigan

Dear Lew:

Than you very much for the information you sent me about
consumer's rights. ·I have read the material, and I am sure that
it will be helpful.

Please let me know if you have any plans to travel this way. I
would like to meet with you and talk about some interests that we
may share.

Sincerely,

Michael Green

P.S. Please find your book enclosed.
                                    Doc 1 Pg 1 Ln 29   Pos 46

Figure 10–1   Letter to Lew

combination to erase the entire line. The post script line should
disappear, and you should be left with the complete letter.

Remember, you could have erased any part of this line by placing the cursor at the point you wanted everything to the right of
deleted.

Deleting a Page

Deleting a page (or part of a page) is just as simple as deleting a
line (or part of a line). To delete page material, do the following:

1. Place the cursor at the point where you want to begin deleting.

2. Press the Ctrl key, and, while holding it down, press the PgDn
    key. When you do this, WordPerfect will give you the following
    message:

Delete Remainder of Page (Y/N)?N

If you want to delete everything on the page from the cursor
on, press the letter Y. If you do not want to delete anything, press
the letter N and WordPerfect will return you to the unchanged
document.

<hr>

WordPerfect Hint

<hr>

An especially useful application of deleting a page is when you begin to write something and find that it just doesn't sound as it should. Simply press the Ctrl→PgDn combination and it's as if you are beginning again with a new piece of typing paper!

But remember, if you use this combination, everything on the page that follows the cursor will be deleted. Fortunately, the deletion does not have to be permanent. Read on!

Clear your WordPerfect screen and recall the file named "comp.rep" that you worked with in lesson 9. Use the PgDn key to move to the top of the second page so your screen looks like figure 10–2.

Now using the cursor arrows, move to the beginning of the first full paragraph, which begins the description of the program called *School Helper*. Place the cursor on the *S*. To erase the remainder of the page, use the Ctrl→PgDn,Y combination. When this combi-

```
unlike what "real" engineers probably do, but it's just alot more
fun.

      School Helper is one of the first multi-purpose integrated
programs developed specifically for children.  In particular,
five Helper tools were designed to help students study more
efficiently.  These all appear to be easy to use and very
helpful.
      The word processor contains many of the features that other
very powerful word processors contain such as moving text to new
locations, wordwrap, and spacing changes.
      The Outliner assists in the organization of notes and allows
the student to change the structure of the outline as ideas
change.
      The Driller creates flash cards on the screen to help in the
drill that is so necessary to master basic math and other skills.
      The Calendar helps students remember important dates,
assignments, tests, and appointments.

      Writing Fun and Math Fun both use wonderful screen graphics
to make the learning of beginning math and writing skills an
enjoyable challenge.
      Writer Fun consists of four games that are sequenced so
                              Doc 1  Pg 1  Ln 27    Pos 10
```

Figure 10–2   Top of Page 2 of Computer Report

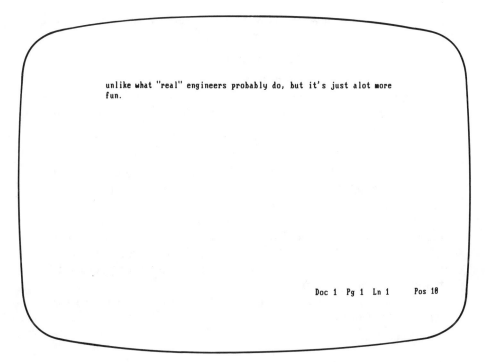

unlike what "real" engineers probably do, but it's just alot more
fun.

Doc 1 Pg 1 Ln 1   Pos 10

Figure 10–3   Erasing the Rest of the Page

nation of keys is pressed, your screen should look like figure 10–3
with the descriptions of the last two computer programs, *School
Helper* and *Writing Fun* and *Math Fun* deleted.

Now, clear your WordPerfect screen (F7,N,N) and move on to
what may be one of WordPerfect's most useful features.

The Undelete Operation

No one is perfect, and try as you might, you'll make mistakes.
Sometimes the mistake is not a simple spelling or error mistake,
but something more drastic, such as erasing a whole page when
you didn't mean to! What to do? Simple. Use the **undelete** command. Undelete actually cancels out up to the last *three* deletions
you made. This means you can **restore** these deletions.

Now while this might sound like the solution to all your problems, beware. The undelete operation will only work on deletions,
and not on other commands. If that last command was to retrieve
a file and you didn't mean to, you can't reverse that action.

The undelete key is the F1 key. For example, clear your screen and recall the file "lew.ltr". Now move to the first line of the second paragraph beginning with the words

Please let me know......

Use the Ctrl→End keys and delete the line.

Oops! You realize you didn't want to delete the line. To undelete the line, press the F1 key to produce the following menu, from which you must choose.

Undelete 1 Restore 2 Show Previous Deletion: 0

When you press the F1 key, the line that you deleted will automatically reappear in reverse video, as you can see in figure 10–4, along with the menu of choices.

If you then select 1, *Restore,* then the reverse video will disappear and what you deleted will be restored. The letter will appear as it did in figure 10–1. If you select 2, WordPerfect will search through previous deletions until it gets to the deletion you want to restore. You can then press 1.

For example, clear your WordPerfect screen, and type in the following list of materials:

1   yellow pads

2.   pens

```
December 2, 1986

Lew Margolin
Consumer's Affairs
1822 West 5th Street
Williams, Michigan

Dear Lew:

Thank you very much for the information you sent me about
consumers' rights. I have read the material, and I am sure
that it will be helpful.

Please let me know if you have any plans to travel this way. I
would like to meet with you and talk about some interests that
we may share.

Sincerely,


Michael Green

P.S. Please find your book enclosed.
Undelete: 1 Restore; 2 Show Previous Deletion: 0
```

Figure 10–4   Highlighted Lines

3. pencils

4. correction fluid

5. magnetic tape

Delete entry 3 by using the Ctrl and End keys. After realizing your mistake, press the F1 key and then the 1 key from the *undelete menu*. You should see the 3 listing of pencils reappear.

You now have the full list of five things. Now delete both the yellow pads (1) and the pens (2) using the Ctrl→End key combination. Now if you undelete them (F1), you can press 2 to show the previous deletions and choose the one you wish to restore. For example, if you realize you don't really need pads, but do need pens, just restore the pens item.

The difference this time is that you should choose the 2 option on the undelete menu so you can page through the previous deletions. When you have found the material you previously deleted that you now want to undelete, press the restore key. You can go back a total of three deletions to correct inadvertent erasures or deletions.

WordPerfect Hint

There's no doubt about it. The WordPerfect undelete option is a powerful tool that can save you hours of work if you accidentally erase an entire page or more! But to avoid even having to use the undelete feature, pause a moment before you erase a large section of a document and ask yourself if this is really what you want to do. In addition, pause before you resave this document. Remember, the original file is still intact on the disk no matter what you do to it on the screen. After you save a document however, what is on your screen is on your disk as well.

Using Blocks

Here's another outstanding feature of WordPerfect. The **block** feature allows you to create a block of text that can be deleted, printed, moved, checked for spelling, and other things as well. A block is a part of a document that is highlighted by WordPerfect so it can be acted on, independent of the document from which it is selected. For example, the following is a block including parts of the last two paragraphs that you just read.

> The **block** feature allows you to create a block of text that can be deleted, printed, moved, checked for spelling, and other things as well. A block is a part of a document that is highlighted by WordPerfect so it can be acted on.

So that you can practice on a document, clear your screen and retrieve the file named "comp.rep". Use the PgDn command to move the cursor to the top of page 2.

To define a block, do the following:

1. Place the cursor at the point you would like to mark the beginning of the block. In this case, move the cursor down to the paragraph that begins with *School Helper,* and place the cursor on the letter *S*.

2. Now press the Alt key, and while holding it down, press the F4 key (Alt→F4).

3. As you can see on your monitor screen, there is a flashing message (Block On) in the bottom left corner of the screen. This tells you that the block feature is operating.

4. Now move your cursor to the end of the block of text you want to identify. In this case it is the word appointments.

As you move the cursor using the arrows, the + key, or the PgDn key, note that the blocked section of text is **highlighted** as shown in figure 10–5.

In this way, you can see exactly what is contained in the block.

You have just identified or highlighted a block of text and are ready to perform any one of several operations on the block. Once a block is defined, it is almost as if you have created a whole new document. You can save a block, print it, delete it, move it, and more. In fact, anything you can do in WordPerfect, can be done on the block level.

Printing a Block

To print a block, press the Shift→F7 combination. WordPerfect will give you the following message:

Print Block (Y/N)? Y

If you want to print the block, just simply press the Y key for yes. If you do not want to print the block, press the N key and you will be returned to the document with the block still highlighted. Press the combination of keys and print the block. You can see how the block is still highlighted on your screen, meaning that the definition of that particular block is still active.

```
more fun.

      School Helper is one of the first multi-purpose integrated
programs developed specifically for children. In particular,
five Helper tools were designed to help students study more
efficiently. These all appear to be easy to use and very
helpful.
      The word processor contains many of the features that other
very powerful word processors contain such as moving text to new
locations, wordwrap, and spacing changes.
      The Outliner assists in the organization of notes and allows
the student to change the structure of the outline as ideas
change.
      The Driller creates flash cards on the screen to help in the
drill that is so necessary to master basic math and other skills.
      The Calendar helps students remember important dates,
assignments, tests, and appointments.

      Writing Fun and Math Fun both use wonderful screen graphics
to make the learning of beginning math and writing skills an
enjoyable challenge.
      Writer Fun consists of four games that are sequenced so
children can start with the recognition of sentences, and proceed
up through the last level that requires completing a story that
Block on                                   Doc 1 Pg 2 Ln 17    Pos 47
```

Figure 10–5   Blocked Area of Text

Saving a Block

Perhaps you need to use this particular set of paragraphs in another report and you would like to save it as a file. This is a very handy feature that allows you to extract text from one document and save it as a unique file (with of course, a unique and different name) for use later.

To save a block, press the F10 key, and WordPerfect will ask you to give the block a name.

Block Name?:

You need to provide a unique (not used before on this disk) name, and WordPerfect will then save it. Use the file name "sh.txt" (for School Helper). When WordPerfect is finished saving the file now named "sh.txt", there will be a new file named sh.txt on your disk. Use the F5 (list files feature) now to check to see that this file is listed.

You will notice that the block is still highlighted and nothing in the original document has been changed. You need to turn off the block, using the Alt→F4 key combination to continue in WordPerfect.

Deleting a Block

There are times, however, where you might want to delete a block from a document. For example, what if *School Helper* was to be excluded from this particular report because it is no longer available?

To delete a block, simply press the Del key. WordPerfect will ask you

Delete Block (Y/N)?N

If you answer yes (press Y), the block will be deleted. If you answer no (press N), you will be returned to the document. Notice how WordPerfect assumes that you do *not* want to erase the block. This is a little warning from WordPerfect that you should think twice before you erase *anything*. If you did erase a block, you can use the F1 undelete feature to restore or recover it.

Once a block is deleted, it is no longer a part of your on-screen document. Remember, that until you save it to the disk on which is was originally recorded, the original copy is still intact.

Before you continue, press the Alt→F4 combination to turn off the block feature.

Moving Text

There's another part of editing that does not involve changing words or correcting misspellings, but is just as important. Often when people write, they find out they need to move a sentence, a paragraph, or even a page (or more) from one place in a document to another. This is done by using the block feature and the **move** feature that WordPerfect offers.

Moving text involves two basic operations. The first is highlighting a block, as you just did. The second is placing the cursor in the location where you want the highlighted block to be moved to. It's that simple and straightforward. For example, the computer software report contains brief descriptions of five different programs for children. The program *Opposites,* however, is not in alphabetical order.

Follow these instructions to move the two paragraphs describing *Opposites* from their current position to a place after the three paragraphs describing the program *Inventions*. They will then be in alphabetical order.

1. Clear your WordPerfect screen and recall the file named "comp.rep". Move the cursor to the first letter of the first word *Opposites* on page 1.

2. Use the Alt and F4 keys to begin a block at

    Opposites is an easy to use. . . .

    and use the cursor keys to end the block at

    . . . .program is set up.

3. Select the Move feature by pressing the Ctrl→F4 combination.
    When this is done, your screen should look like figure 10–6, with the block highlighted and the move menu running across the bottom of the screen.

    As you can see, there are five different items on that menu. When you chose any one of the five, WordPerfect will know to perform the operation that you have selected on the block that you have just identified.
    The five options are
    Cut block (option 1) will cut the block out of the document and store it in temporary memory until you tell WordPerfect where you want to put it. Once it is cut out of a document it is removed permanently from the document, unless you restore using the undelete option.

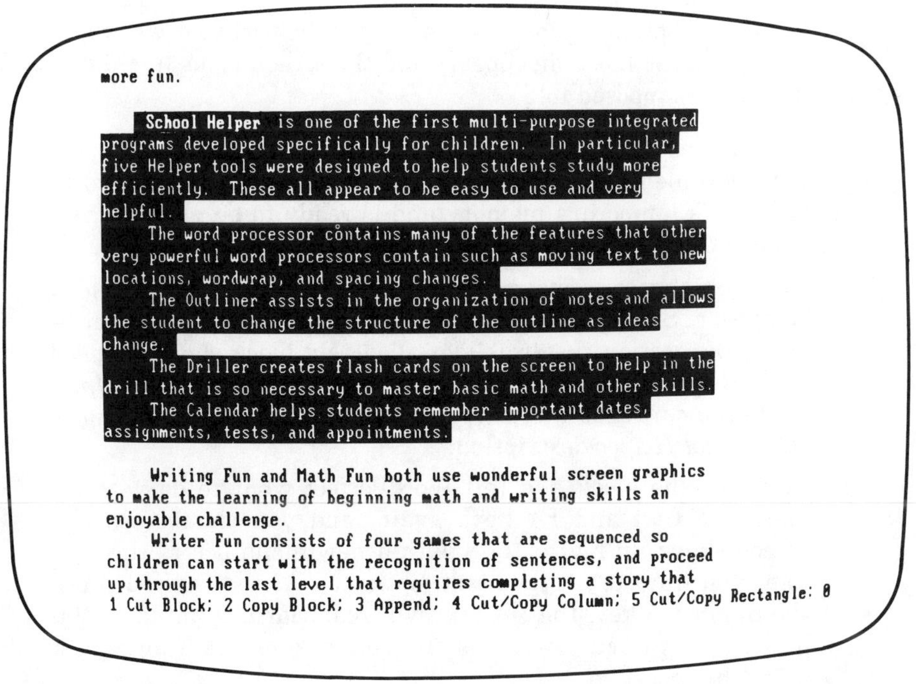

more fun.

    School Helper is one of the first multi-purpose integrated programs developed specifically for children. In particular, five Helper tools were designed to help students study more efficiently. These all appear to be easy to use and very helpful.
    The word processor contains many of the features that other very powerful word processors contain such as moving text to new locations, wordwrap, and spacing changes.
    The Outliner assists in the organization of notes and allows the student to change the structure of the outline as ideas change.
    The Driller creates flash cards on the screen to help in the drill that is so necessary to master basic math and other skills.
    The Calendar helps students remember important dates, assignments, tests, and appointments.

    Writing Fun and Math Fun both use wonderful screen graphics to make the learning of beginning math and writing skills an enjoyable challenge.
    Writer Fun consists of four games that are sequenced so children can start with the recognition of sentences, and proceed up through the last level that requires completing a story that
1 Cut Block; 2 Copy Block; 3 Append; 4 Cut/Copy Column; 5 Cut/Copy Rectangle; 0

Figure 10–6   Blocked Area with Move Menu

This is the option you should choose if you want to move something from one part of a document to another, and only want it to appear in one place.

Copy block (option 2) will copy the block to another part of the document, but the blocked text will also remain in the same location.

This is a handy tool if you want to repeat a certain section of text, such as a name or address, in different places.

Append block (option 3) allows you to add the identified block to the end of another file. For example, if you were writing several reports and wanted the information in the block on the program called *Opposites* to appear in another file, you could append this block to the other file.

Cut/Copy Column and **Cut/Copy Rectangle** (options 4 and 5) are special WordPerfect features that allow you to move columns and rectangles from one place to another. These functions are designed for work on columnar text (mostly often numbers) and text, such as report headings, that is rectangular in shape.

4. For the example presented here, you should choose option 1 since you want to *cut* from one part of a document and place it in another. In other words, you no longer want it to appear where it now does.

    Select option 1. Don't be alarmed if the text that was highlighted in the block disappears and the screen looks like figure 10–7. It's supposed to!

As you can see in figure 10–7, the text was completely removed from the document. What you can't see is that this text is stored in WordPerfect's temporary memory and is ready to be placed wherever you choose.

5. The next step is to move the cursor where you want the block to appear. Since your objective is to alphabetize these descriptions, the section that was identified as a block should appear after the description of *Inventions* and before *School Helper*. Move the cursor down to the line right before the beginning of the *School Helper* description.

6. To recall the block and tell WordPerfect what to do with it, press the Ctrl and F4 keys again, and you should see the screen shown in figure 10–8 with a new menu across the bottom. You want to retrieve text (option 5). As soon as you press the number 5 key, the cut text will reappear beginning at the location of the cursor. Press the return and the Tab key to align the insertion.

The descriptions are now in alphabetical order, as shown in figure 10–9.

```
    types of brakes lends lots of excitement, potential and reality
    of the design and testing process.


            Inventions is really one of those toys you buy for the kids
    but end up using it yourself.  With it, you can learn about
    mechanical principles by actually constructing gizmos that use
    pulleys, springs, and magnets.  These are combined with some
    wacky characters and objects on the screen to develop what can
    only be called Rube Goldberg "lookalikes".
            The four main activities Mechanism Review, Fill In
    Mechanisms, Fill In Zany Objects, and Contraption Mix Up provide
    instruction on how the Creative Contraptions work and what you
    can do with them.
            Besides being fun however, it does encourage you to learn
    about planning in advance and the development of systems that
    work.  Otherwise, Creative Contraptions lets you know that
    something is amiss and won't continue, but instead send you back
    to the beginning of your project.  Creative Contraptions is not
    unlike what "real" engineers probably do, but it's just allot
    more fun.

            School Helper is one of the first multi-purpose integrated
```

Figure 10–7   Blocked Area "Cut"

Quick Moves

There is the another set of options (1, 2, and 3) on the same move menu (in figure 10–8) that are very handy. These can be used to move things by *automatically* blocking a sentence, paragraph, or page.

Be sure that your WordPerfect screen is cleared, and type in the following paragraphs.

There are five things that you need to complete in order to be considered for the honors program. They are as follows.
1) Attend the orientation session for new students.
2) Submit a letter of application.
3) Submit a complete manuscript.
4) Provide two letters of recommendation.
5) Sign up for one extra-curricular activity.
Once you have completed these materials, your application
will be considered and you will be contacted within six weeks.

The fourth requirement needs to be moved to the top of list, and the list renumbered.

To do this, follow these steps.

```
types of brakes lends lots of excitement, potential and reality
of the design and testing process.


        Inventions is really one of those toys you buy for the kids
but end up using it yourself.  With it, you can learn about
mechanical principles by actually constructing gizmos that use
pulleys, springs, and magnets.  These are combined with some
wacky characters and objects on the screen to develop what can
only be called Rube Goldberg "lookalikes".
        The four main activities Mechanism Review, Fill In
Mechanisms, Fill In Zany Objects, and Contraption Mix Up provide
instruction on how the Creative Contraptions work and what you
can do with them.
        Besides being fun however, it does encourage you to learn
about planning in advance and the development of systems that
work.  Otherwise, Creative Contraptions lets you know that
something is amiss and won't continue, but instead send you back
to the beginning of your project.  Creative Contraptions is not
unlike what "real" engineers probably do, but it's just allot
more fun.

        School Helper is one of the first multi-purpose integrated
Move 1 Sentence; 2 Paragraph; 3 Page; Retrieve 4 Column; 5 Text; 6 Rectangle: 0
```

Figure 10–8   The Move/Retrieve Menu

1. Place the cursor at the beginning of the sentence, paragraph, or page that you want to move. In this case, it is item 4.

2. Select the *move* feature by using the Ctrl and F4 keys. You will notice that you have not identified a block of any kind.

3. Select option 1, which, in this case, automatically creates a block of the sentence and gives you the following two choices:

1) Cut; 2) Copy: 0

As before, if you select option 1, the identified text (now as a block) will be removed from the document to be placed somewhere else. Select option 1. If you choose option 2, the identified text will be saved to be copied somewhere else.

4. Now move the cursor to where you want the text to appear. In this example, it should be placed first on the list.

5. Now select the move menu again (Ctrl→F4) and then select option 5 to move the text to the designated spot. The text should look like this:

```
      Inventions is really one of those toys you buy for the kids
 but end up using it yourself.  With it, you can learn about
 mechanical principles by actually constructing gizmos that use
 pulleys, springs, and magnets.  These are combined with some
 wacky characters and objects on the screen to develop what can
 only be called Rube Goldberg "lookalikes".
      The four main activities Mechanism Review, Fill In
 Mechanisms, Fill In Zany Objects, and Contraption Mix Up provide
 instruction on how the Creative Contraptions work and what you
 can do with them.
      Besides being fun however, it does encourage you to learn
 about planning in advance and the development of systems that
 work.  Otherwise, Creative Contraptions lets you know that
 something is amiss and won't continue, but instead send you back
 to the beginning of your project.  Creative Contraptions is not
 unlike what "real" engineers probably do, but it's just allot
 more fun.

      Opposites is an easy to use program for preschoolers that is
 full of entertaining graphics and sound.  After the software is
 loaded, a series of engaging and colorful screens presents one of
 two words such as tall or fast or empty. Using the joystick or
                                          Doc 1  Pg 1  Ln 51     Pos 15
```

Figure 10–9   Descriptions in Alphabetical Order

There are five things that you need to complete in order to be considered for the honors program. They are as follows.

4) Provide two letters of recommendation.

1) Attend the orientation session for new students.

2) Submit a letter of application.

3) Submit a complete manuscript.

5) Sign up for one extra-curricular activity.

Once you have completed these materials, your application will be considered and you will be contacted within six weeks.

Now, all that needs to be done is renumbering the list and then deleting the space left between the "3)" and the "5)" (using the Del key).

This quick move feature is especially useful if you want to move entire paragraphs or pages, since you do not need to move the cursor to create the block. The move option automatically creates the block for you whether it be a sentence, paragraph, or page.

Since you already have this memo typed in, and you have just renumbered the list, try and use the quick move feature to move

the last paragraph beginning with *Once you have. . . ..* to follow
the first paragraph so the final document looks like this.

> There are five things that you need to complete in order to be
> considered for the honors program. They are as follows. Once
> you have completed these materials, your application will be
> considered and you will be contacted within six weeks.
> 1) Provide two letters of recommendation.
> 2) Attend the orientation session for new students.
> 3) Submit a letter of application.
> 4) Submit a complete manuscript.
> 5) Sign up for one extra-curricular activity.

Notice that, in this example, the second paragraph was combined with the first.

WordPerfect Hint

*The quick move feature is very helpful and can
save time and keystrokes. But it can create some
problems. For example, WordPerfect looks for a
period to define a sentence. If you should have
something in your text like*

Dr. Fine will be available for consultation on May 23
between 8 A.M. and 10 A.M.,

*it will treat everything from the period ending
the previous sentence to the abbreviation* Dr. *as a
sentence! When in doubt, block and move. If not,
use the quick move feature.*

LESSON 10 EXERCISES

1. Type in the following set of sentences exactly as they appear.
   a) There is no difference between the first and second.
   b) There is no difference   the first and second.
                between

   Now using the Ctrl→End combination, delete the last three words of sentence a.

   Now using the block feature, delete the last three words of sentence b.

   Can you think of any general rules for when it is better to delete line by line rather than using the block feature?

2. What are five examples where you would use the block feature of WordPerfect to copy text from one document to another?

3. In the following paragraph, where would you place the cursor if you wanted to move the second sentence to the top of the paragraph?

   He decided that it was not the right kind of position for him at this time. The other jobs he applied for were all more attractive.

   What would be the sequence of keystrokes to do this move?

4. How many accidental deletions can you undelete using WordPerfect? Provide an example where you might need to delete more than one level and then recover text.

5. Recall the file titled "comm.mem".
   a) Use the block feature and delete from line 8 through line 14.
   b) Use the end of page feature and delete the last sentence in the memo.
   c) Use the delete end of line feature and delete the last two categories (d. and e.) on the list.

6. With the file titled "comm.mem" on the screen, cut and move the list of committees to *after* the last line of the memo ending with the word *yourself*.

7. Clear your WordPerfect screen and select the file "link1". Now append this file to the end of the file named "lew.ltr". Clear your WordPerfect screen and recall the file "lew.ltr" and delete the name Michael Green.

8. Write out the sequence of keys that you would use to define a block and use it to create a new file.

9. Delete the dates from the "sales.dat" file and insert today's date. Save the file under its new name.

LESSON 11
Searching and Replacing Text

After this lesson you'll know

- How to search for a specific character, word, or phrase.
- How to search forward and backward throughout a document.
- What global search and replace means.
- How to search for and change one occurrence or several.
- How to use the block feature and search feature to move a block to another part of a document.

Important Terms

backward search	global search and	replace
forward search	replace	search

Important Keys

Alt→F2	F2	Shift→F2

Imagine this. You have just finished writing a 15-page paper and spelling the word *committee* 27 times with only one "m", as *comittee*! Or, you spelled the word *interpersonal* without the hyphen, rather then *inter-personal* 18 times!

There are two things that you can do when this happens. The first is to go through the paper and change each individual occurrence of the error. The second, and the one you'll learn about in this lesson, is to have WordPerfect **search** through the report and *automatically* change every word or phrase you want.

Begin this lesson by making sure that your WordPerfect screen is cleared.

Searching Through a Document

WordPerfect allows you to search through a document to find a character, word, or set of words up to 59 spaces long. If you wanted to, you could ask WordPerfect to change words such as *house* or *food*, to phrases such as *contemporary house* or *fast food*, or to sentences such as "He lives in a contemporary house" or "She likes fast food."

You can search **forward** from the beginning of a document to the end of a document, or you can search **backward** from the end of a document to the beginning. You can even search and automatically **replace** all occurrences, or have WordPerfect stop and wait when it finds what you are searching for and ask you if want to change it or skip over it.

The memo in figure 11–1 contains several words that are consistently misspelled as well as other phrases that need to be changed. This memo will be the practice file for this lesson.

Searching Forward

The dean recently changed the policy regarding how many committees people need to serve on and needed to change the wording in the memo from *three* to *two* to reflect the change. Before a word (or a letter or a phrase) can be changed, it must be located. Follow these steps to search forward and find a set of characters. Be sure that your WordPerfect screen is cleared.

1. Recall the file named "comm.mem".

2. Move the cursor to the beginning of the document.

3. Press the F2 key and you will see in the bottom left-hand corner of your screen the message

$\rightarrow$ Srch:

```
                              M E M O

             To: All teaching faculty chairs
             From: The Dean
             Re: Assignment to comittees

             As you know, each member of your department, is responsible for
             serving on three comittees each year.  This is to ensure that
             all faculty have a say in what policies are set and what types of
             work comittees focus on.


             The comittees are as follows:

                  a. Resource Comittee
                  b. Promotion and Tenure Comittee
                  c. Grievance Comittee
                  d. Staff Benefits Comittee
                  e. Social and Recreation Comittee

             Please be sure to solicit membership for each of the three as
             well as contributing time yourself.
```

Figure 11–1   Committee Memo with Errors

4. Enter the word *three*, so the message line looks as follows:

    → Srch: three

5. Now, press the F2 key again, and WordPerfect will take you to the end of the word *three*. Now use the left cursor arrow to move to the beginning of the word.
    You can now delete the word *three*:

    Ctrl→BackSpace

and type in the word *two* and a space. You have just searched forward, located, and changed a word.

The word *three*, however, occurs again. Fortunately, WordPerfect remembers what you searched for last time. By just pressing the F2 key twice, you will find that WordPerfect brings you to the next occurrence of the word *three*.

WordPerfect Hint

WordPerfect will always search for the last entered set of characters when F2 is pressed, unless you enter a different set.

Do not save the changes you made in this memo, but clear your WordPerfect screen.

Searching Backward

Suppose, however, that you are at the end of a document and you want to search for a set of characters without first going back to the top or the beginning. This may be especially useful if the change that you want to make is towards the end of a long document. This can be easily accomplished using the search backward WordPerfect feature that uses the Shift→F2 combination of keys.

To search backward, follow these steps:

1. Retrieve the "comm.mem" file.

2. Go to the end of the "comm.mem" file (using the Home,Home,Down arrow cursor key combination).

3. Press the Shift key and, while holding it down, press the F2 key. The message you will see at the bottom of your screen is

← Srch: three

4. Now press the F2 key and WordPerfect will search backward and find the word *three*.

What if you wanted to search for a different set of characters? For example, what if you have just found out that the name of the Promotion and Tenure committee has been changed to Promotions Committee? Return to the top of the document and press the F2 key to begin the search forward function. You'll again see the word *three* being searched for, since WordPerfect remembers the last set of characters.

As soon as you start typing in the new set of characters you want WordPerfect to search for, the previous set of characters (*three*) disappears. The search message should now look like this:

Srch→: Promotion

Now press the F2 key. WordPerfect will take you to the end of the word *Promotion*, where you can begin to make whatever changes you need.

If WordPerfect cannot find the set of characters to change, it will give you this message:

* Not Found *

For example, go to the top of the memo, and search for the word *fact*. You'll shortly see the * *Not Found* * message in the lower left corner of your monitor screen.

WordPerfect Hint

When you search for a character, a word, or a set of words, be careful that you give WordPerfect enough information to find what you are looking for. For example, if you needed to add an additional committee name to the list in the memo, you could search for the letter e *(since this is the last letter in the name of the last committee on the list). But, because there are so many other* es *that occur in the memo, you would have to go through each one until you find the one you want to place new information after.*

Rather than search for something that is very common, look for a unique set of characters. In this case, the set could be the characters e. S, *which are part of the longer set of characters, e.* Social and Recreation Committee. *It's highly unlikely that this particular set of characters is repeated in another place in the document. Searching for this sequence will bring you to place where you can add a new committee. You could then go to the end of that line, press the return key, and add a new committee.*

Searching and Inserting

Searching forward and backwards have many uses. Most often they are used to find set of characters that need to be changed, or an area of a report that needs to be edited. For example, you may use the search feature to find a location where new material needs to be inserted. Let's say you wanted to add another paragraph to the children's software report that you worked with earlier. The new paragraph will be placed after the first paragraph in the report.

The sequence of steps would be as follows. Be sure that your screen is clear.

1. Recall the file named "comp.rep".
2. Go to the end of the document.
3. Write the new paragraph.
4. Create a block of the new paragraph.
5. Cut the new block to be moved (Ctrl→F4,1).
6. Use the Shift→F2 key combination to search backward and

find the words *sales period.* (the place you want to move the new block).

7. Press the return key to go to a new line.

8. Insert the new block (Ctrl→F4,5).

WordPerfect Hint

When a block is cut or copied, it remains in the computer's memory while you search backward or forward for where you want to place the block. It will remain in temporary memory until you call it out again, using the Ctrl→F4,5 sequence of commands.

Searching and Replacing Text

WordPerfect offers a variety of ways to locate and change something in one step.

In the example of the committee memo (figure 11–1), you may have noticed that the word *committee* was spelled incorrectly nine times. You need to change every occurrence of *comittee* to *committee.*

To make what is called a **global search and replace,** follow these steps. Be sure that your WordPerfect screen is clear.

1. Retrieve the file named "comm.mem" (shown in figure 11–1).

2. Press the Alt→F2 combination and you will see the following message on the bottom of the screen

w/Confirm? (Y/N) N

WordPerfect is asking you whether you would like to stop at each incorrect spelling and have the chance to say "Yes, I want to replace the word," or "No, I do not want to, *only for that one occurrence*".

There are times when you may not want to automatically replace all the occurrences of a certain word. For example, what if you inadvertently typed a period in the middle of a word, such as *docu.ment* instead of *document*? In this case, you certainly do not want to find every occurrence of a period, and change it to a blank space! You would end up with a hopeless mess of text without periods. Instead, you would want Word-Perfect to stop and let you decide whether the change is needed for the particular occurrence. In this example, you want all occurrences to be changed, so press the return key indicating *no.*

3. WordPerfect then requests the set of characters you want to search for. Type in the word *comittee* (the incorrect spelling), so the message line on your screen looks as follows:

→ srch: comittee

press the F2. Remember, you must search for exactly what is there. If you type in *committee* (the correct spelling), WordPerfect will not be able to find it. Although WordPerfect is wonderful, it does not yet think for itself.

4. WordPerfect then asks you what you want to replace this set of characters with, and you should type in the correct spelling of the word. The next complete message line appears as:

Replace with: committee

Pressing the F2 key activates the search and each occurrence of the word *comittee* is replaced with *committee.*
The final memo, with all the changes made, appears in figure 11–2.

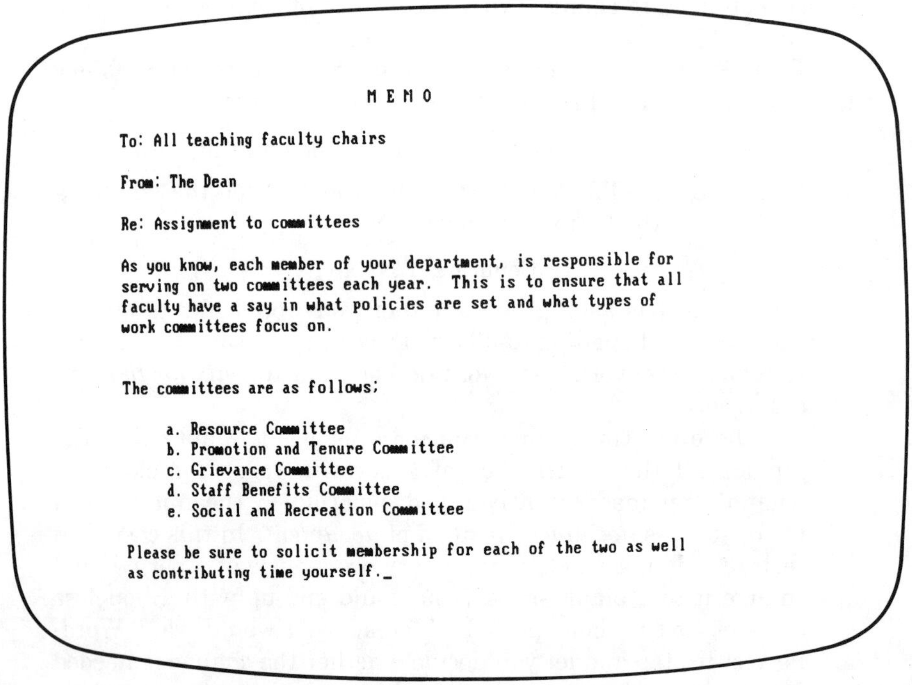

M E M O

To: All teaching faculty chairs

From: The Dean

Re: Assignment to committees

As you know, each member of your department, is responsible for serving on two committees each year. This is to ensure that all faculty have a say in what policies are set and what types of work committees focus on.

The committees are as follows;

a. Resource Committee
b. Promotion and Tenure Committee
c. Grievance Committee
d. Staff Benefits Committee
e. Social and Recreation Committee

Please be sure to solicit membership for each of the two as well as contributing time yourself._

Figure 11–2 Corrected Committee Memo

Remember that you can search, and search and replace, through an entire document, or just through a block of text that you have previously identified. For example, if you wanted to change the word *grievance* to *complaint*, you could form a block of only the five listed committees and then perform the search and replace function.

LESSON 11 EXERCISES

1. What would happen if you spelled the word *the* as *thw*, and asked WordPerfect to find *w* and change it to *e*?

2. Here are some words and phrases that need to be changed. Write down next to each one, the sequence of commands that you would use to change them. Some of them need spelling changes, but others require you to work with spacing and punctuation.

- change *face* to *fact*
- change *this child* to *that child*
- change *at the end. This* to *at the beginning. This*
- change ***The End*** to ****The End****
- change

  This is the only person whom I know. to
     This is the only person whom I know.

3. Provide an example of when you might search forward through a document to find something and when you might use the backward search option.

4. In a search and replace operation, what is one example of when your answer to the WordPerfect question

                    w/Confirm? (Y/N) N

   would be Y (for *yes*)?

5. Clear your WordPerfect screen and type in the following list:
   a. nails
   b. screws
   c. lumber
   d. twine
   e. wood glue

   Now rearrange the list to look like this:
   a.   nails
   b.   screws
   c.   lumber
   d.   twine
   e.   wood glue

6. For the following phrases or sentences, indicate what string, or set of letters or words, you would enter to search for the incorrect spelling. Be sure that you enter unique information.
   a) he is hte one
   b) I od not know.
   c) What a suprise it was to see Bill at the party.

d) Even though he graduated with the rest of his class,

e) There were two many people at the meeting.

7. Write out the sequence of keystrokes it would take to transform list A into list B.

List A	List B
toys	balls
trains	candy
candy	games
games	toys
balls	trains

8. Here is the first paragraph from the file named "comp.rep" with a misspelled word in the first line.

In changing the word *raelly* to *really,* why wouldn't you use the global search and replace feature to change the *a* to an *e* and then the *e* to an *a*? What is the proper set of commands to correct the spelling?

Here are some of the *raelly* outstanding children's and family software that I have come across in the last few months during my marketing activities. We should seriously consider making them part of regular offerings to our customers. Most of them are reasonably priced, readily available, and may be successful items, especially during the holiday sales period.

LESSON 12
Formatting Your Documents

After this lesson you'll know

- Why formatting a text properly is so important.
- The available WordPerfect formatting options.
- What reveal codes are and how they are used.
- How reveal codes can be changed and deleted.
- How to underline text.
- How to bold text.
- How to center text.

Important Terms

bold	italics	reformat
center	line format	reveal codes
default values	page format	underline
font	print format	WYSIWYG
format		

Important Keys

Alt→F3	F8	Shift→F6
F6		

The Importance of Formatting

Often, how memos, letters, and reports look is almost as important as what they say. A letter that is well organized, but poorly **formatted,** doesn't have the punch that a good piece of communication needs. You might want to run off a quick note to a friend, but an important letter or your resume and job application should have as much visual appeal as possible.

Look at the simple letter in figure 12–1. It does not convey the importance of the message. The spacing is incorrect and inconsistent, and characters are not properly aligned.

Look at the revision of the letter in figure 12–2. Here the margins have been changed, the right-hand edge of the letter is irregular (which may be visually more appealing than when it is all even), and the spacing is consistent. You can see by this simple illustration that text format should be uncluttered in its presentation and easy on the eye of the reader.

Formatting and WordPerfect

There are three general categories of format changes that you can make in a WordPerfect document.

The first is **line format** changes. These deal with changes such as the length and spacing between lines. The second is **page format** changes. These deal with changes such as page length and page number location. The third category of changes is **print format** changes. These deal with changes such as the actual appearance of the print on the page, including how many letters per inch are printed and the **font** or typeface used.

In the next three lessons, you will learn how to make these line, page, and print format changes. Before you begin, there are some general things that you need to remember about how WordPerfect formats documents.

First, any new format commands change the format of only the text that follows the command. For example, you can see how this part of the paragraph is single spaced, while the first two lines of the paragraph are double spaced.

Second, WordPerfect is a **WYSIWYG** word processor. WYSIWYG stands for "What You See Is What You Get". The way that the text appears on the monitor screen is the way that it appears on the printed copy. This allows you to work with the text until the format matches your needs exactly and it lets you see what the final product will look like *before* you print it.

Third, once a format command is initiated, WordPerfect auto-

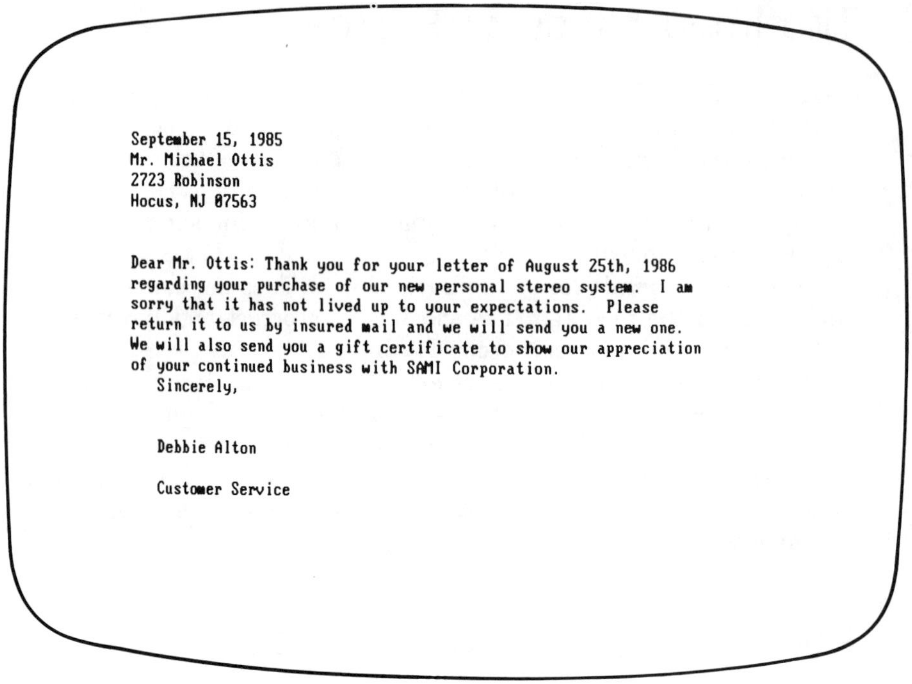

September 15, 1985
Mr. Michael Ottis
2723 Robinson
Hocus, NJ 87563

Dear Mr. Ottis: Thank you for your letter of August 25th, 1986
regarding your purchase of our new personal stereo system. I am
sorry that it has not lived up to your expectations. Please
return it to us by insured mail and we will send you a new one.
We will also send you a gift certificate to show our appreciation
of your continued business with SAMI Corporation.
   Sincerely,

Debbie Alton

Customer Service

Figure 12–1   A Poorly Formatted Letter

matically **reformats** the entire document. If you change the spacing from single to double, or change the left margin from 10 to 20 spaces, *all* of the text that follows the format command will be changed as well. Many word processors only reformat one paragraph at a time. WordPerfect saves you time and effort by automatically reformatting the entire document.

Finally, as with other WordPerfect features, there are the **default values** mentioned earlier. These are preset formatting commands that are automatically in place each time you begin using WordPerfect. For example, when you begin a new document, the left-hand margin will always be set at 10 spaces, the right-hand margin will always be set at 70 spaces and the text will be single spaced unless you change these preset values. As you go through the line, page, and print format menus, you'll learn what these default settings are.

Using Reveal Codes

As you will learn in this lesson, WordPerfect has some very special and powerful tools for changing the appearance of your document.

```
September 15, 1986

Mr. Michael Ottis
2723 Robinson
Hocus, NJ 87563

Dear Mr. Ottis:

Thank you for your letter of August 25th, 1986 regarding your
purchase of our new personal stereo system.  I am sorry that it
has not lived up to your expectations.
Please return it to us by insured mail and we will send you a new
one.

We will also send you a gift certificate to show our appreciation
for your continued business with SAMI Corporation.

Sincerely,


Debbie Alton
Customer Service
```

Figure 12–2   A Well-Formatted Letter

One thing that WordPerfect doesn't do, however, and for good reason, is show the actual codes that control the format on your monitor screen. That is, when you enter a specific command to change something, the actual *code* itself will not appear on the screen, but instead, it is *hidden*. In WordPerfect, these hidden codes are called **reveal codes**.

Why are they hidden? The main reason is the appearance of many different codes that are used to indicate formatting changes in a document would make the screen crowded and unreadable. Take, for example, the split screen shown in figure 12–3. Here is some simple WordPerfect text with the reveal codes showing in the lower half of the screen. You can see how much more difficult it is to read the lower half of the screen than the upper half.

The ideal situation, then, would be to have all of these reveal codes available when you want them, but not to have them appear as a regular feature of the WordPerfect screen. This is exactly the way this WordPerfect feature is designed.

By pressing the key combination Alt→F3 your WordPerfect screen will be split into two screens, as you can see in figure 12–3. The top part will contain a portion of the text, and the bottom part will contain the same text but will also include all the reveal codes

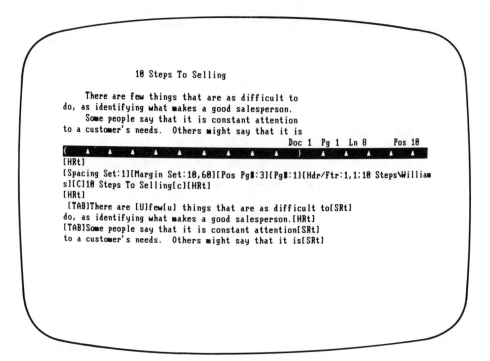

```
                  10 Steps To Selling

        There are few things that are as difficult to
   do, as identifying what makes a good salesperson.
        Some people say that it is constant attention
   to a customer's needs.  Others might say that it is
                                           Doc 1  Pg 1  Ln 8        Pos 10
   {   ▲   ▲   ▲   ▲   ▲   ▲   ▲   ▲   ▲   ▲   }   ▲   ▲   ▲   ▲   ▲
   [HRt]
   [Spacing Set:1][Margin Set:10,60][Pos Pg#:3][Pg#:1][Hdr/Ftr:1,1;10 Steps\William
   s][C]10 Steps To Selling[c][HRt]
   [HRt]
    [TAB]There are [U]few[u] things that are as difficult to[SRt]
   do, as identifying what makes a good salesperson.[HRt]
   [TAB]Some people say that it is constant attention[SRt]
   to a customer's needs.  Others might say that it is[SRt]
```

Figure 12–3   An Example of Split Screen with Reveal Codes

that deal with everything from the number of spaces between lines
and the position of page numbers to what words will be underlined
and how. While the screen with the reveal codes might look a little
intimidating, through some practice, you'll find that it is easy to
understand and use.

An Example of Reveal Codes

WordPerfect uses more than 75 different kinds of reveal codes. In
WordPerfect Extras, there is a listing of all of the reveal codes and
what they represent. Most of these reveal codes are almost self-
explanatory. For example, the reveal code [Spacing Set:2] means
the text will be double spaced.

In figure 12–4, you can see just 10 of these reveal codes; each
is numbered. Read about what each one means as you match it up
with the explanation given below.

1.   [Spacing Set:1] - Place one space between lines.

2.   [Margin Set:10,60] - Set the margins at 10 for the left-hand
     margin and 60 for the right-hand margin.

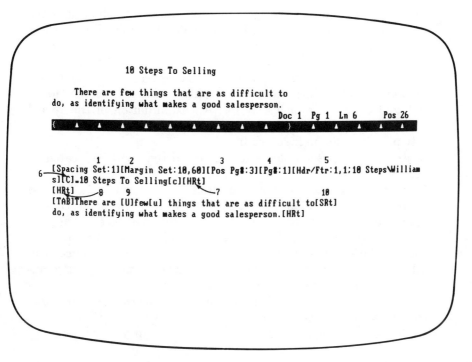

Figure 12–4   10 Reveal Codes

3. [Pos Pg#:3] - Put page numbers in position three, which is the upper right-hand corner of each page.

4. [Pg#:1] - This sets the new page number to be 1.

5. [Hdr/Ftr:1,1;..] - Place a "header" at the top of each page written as "10 Steps/Williams".

6. [C]. . .[c] - Center the Words 10 Steps to. . . .

7. [HRt] - This is a "hard carriage" return, or one that you enter by pressing the return key.

8. [Tab] - This is a tab setting.

9. [U] [u] - These indicate which characters will be underlined.

10. [SRt] - This is a "soft carriage" return, or the kind that WordPerfect automatically inserts when it uses its word wrap feature.

How to Use Reveal Codes

There are a few things that will help you in using reveal codes. First, they are the first thing to check if your text does not format correctly. Press the Alt→F3 combination and see if you really have entered what you intended to. For example, clear your WordPerfect screen and recall the file named "reveal.ex". Now activate the reveal codes feature, Alt→F3. As you can see in figure 12–5, the first two lines of this paragraph are double spaced, but the writer wanted the entire paragraph single spaced. (You'll learn how to set and control spacing in lesson 14). An examination of the reveal codes shows that a double-space code [Spacing Set:2] was mistakenly placed *after* the first two lines.

Wherever the cursor is located, the reveal code will be located as well.

Second, if the text is not formatting the way you want, you can delete a reveal code, just as you delete any other character. Simply use the delete or the backspace keys. Do this with the spacing reveal code from figure 12–5 on the screen. Move the cursor to after the reveal code for spacing and press the back space key once. You will see how the format on the screen adjusts to the default condition of single spacing as shown in figure 12–6.

Finally, remember that when you save your WordPerfect file, you are also saving all of the reveal codes that go along with it.

Remember, reveal codes are a tool to help you better "see"

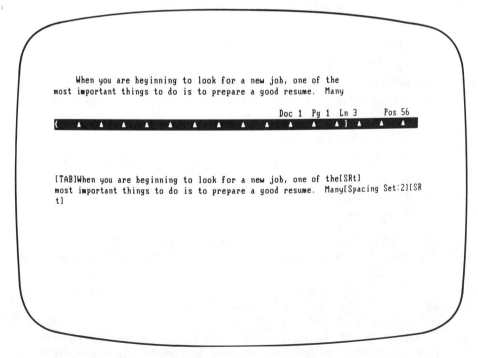

Figure 12–5   The Double-Spaced Reveal Code

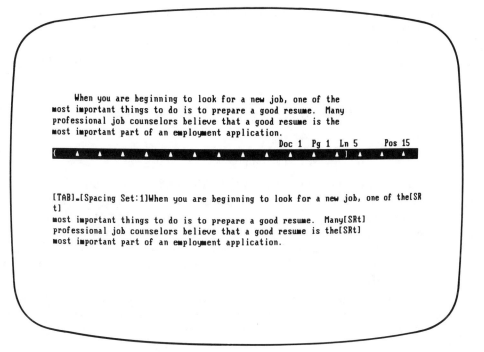

When you are beginning to look for a new job, one of the
most important things to do is to prepare a good resume. Many
professional job counselors believe that a good resume is the
most important part of an employment application.
                                        Doc 1 Pg 1 Ln 5   Pos 15

[TAB]_[Spacing Set:1]When you are beginning to look for a new job, one of the[SR
t]
most important things to do is to prepare a good resume. Many[SRt]
professional job counselors believe that a good resume is the[SRt]
most important part of an employment application.

Figure 12–6   Single-Spaced Text

what you are doing with your WordPerfect document. Checking
them every now and then will help insure that your text is formatted the way you want. One excellent way to practice using reveal
codes is to check them each time you make the kinds of format
changes that follow in this lesson and in lessons 13 and 14.

Using Underlining and Bold

Underlining

There are two ways to underline WordPerfect text, whether it is a
character, a word, or an entire paragraph. The first way is to press
the F8 key where you want underlining to begin, and then to press
the F8 key again where you want it to stop. This is the most used
method when you know what you want underlined *before* you begin entering text.

However, you may sometimes type in some text and, *after* the
fact, want to go back and underline a portion of it. If you want to
underline text that has already been entered, use the block com-

mand (see lesson 10) to block the text you want underlined, and then press the F8 key.

For example, in the following sentence, two words (know it) should be underlined. The first step is to block the two words. The second step is to press the F8 key.

Step 1

> The best way to sell a product is to first know it!

Step 2

> The best way to sell a product is to first <u>know it</u>!

On a color monitor, you may see the underlined words highlighted in a contrasting color. A monochrome monitor may show the underlining. On some monitors, the actual underlining will not show up. In any case, you can see where the underlining begins and ends by checking the reveal codes. The two words *know it*, will have the reveal codes [U] and [u] surrounding them, as shown in figure 12–7.

If you are using a color monitor, you will notice that the underlined text appears in a different color than the other text, and

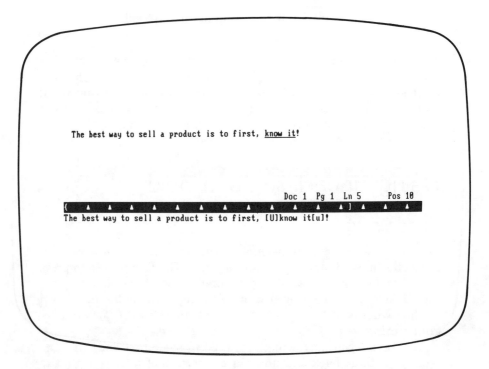

Figure 12–7   An Example of Underlining with Reveal Codes

that the character position indicator of the cursor (lesson 3) also changes color until you are done underlining.

Bolding

The same two options that are available for underlining are also available for bolding. Where the F8 key was used for underlining, the F6 key is used to bold text. For example, in this sentence, **the last seven words appear in bold**. (But not the period at the end!) If you look at the reveal codes as shown in figure 12–8, you will see the seven words surrounded by the [B] and the [b] reveal codes.

If you are using a color monitor, you will notice that the bolded text appears in a different color than the other text, and that the character position indicator of the cursor (lesson 3) changes to the same color until you are done bolding.

When to Use Underline and Bold

Underline and bold are both used for emphasis or to make certain words or phrases stand out. You can use both interchangeably, but keep the following in mind. First, if you use them too much, they

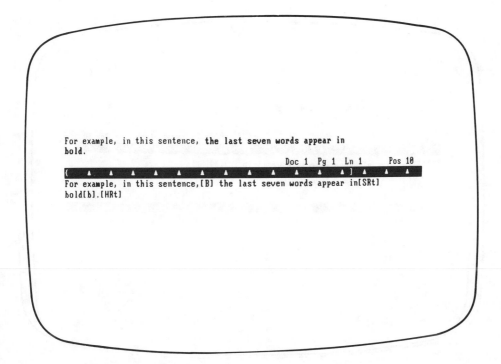

Figure 12–8   An Example of Bolding with Reveal Codes

will lose their power to get the reader to notice what you want to emphasize. In other words, don't underline every other word! Second, underlining can have a special meaning. When documents are professionally typeset and printed, the underlined words are printed in **italics**. So, if you want your words printed in italics, underline them in the draft copy. Finally, the bold feature is used to highlight a section heading, such as in an outline. The underlining feature is more often used for emphasizing text.

Centering Words and Text

There are also two ways to **center** words and text using WordPerfect. The first is to use the combination Shift→F6, which automatically moves the cursor to the middle of the page. When you type in text, it is then automatically centered. This option should be used when you are centering new text.

For example, here is the title of a report. It is not only centered, but also bolded for emphasis.

The Uses of Video Tape in Advertising

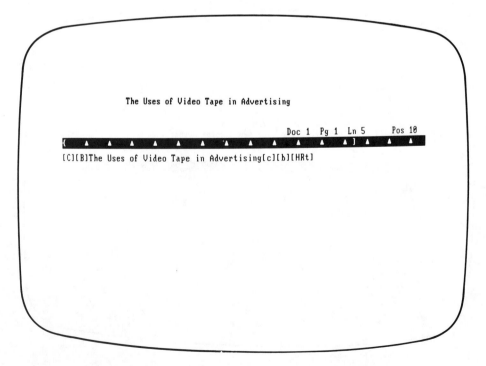

Figure 12–9   An Example of Bolding and Centering

The title *with* reveal codes showing for both centering and bold are shown in figure 12–9.

When you have text to be centered that has already been entered, centering takes a few more steps. To center already entered text, do the following:

1. Place the cursor on the first letter of the line to be centered.

2. Now press the Shift→F6 combination. The text should move to the right-hand side of the screen.

3. Now press the down cursor arrow key and the text should be centered.

_____

WordPerfect Hint

_____

If your text does not center after you follow the above three steps, try the following. First, use the Alt→F3 combination to show the reveal codes and delete any center codes for that line. Sometimes, more than one center code is entered on adjacent lines. Now, try to center the line again. Remember, that unlike underlining and bolding, you do not use the block feature of WordPerfect when you are centering.

LESSON 12 EXERCISES

1. Look at the following letter to an editor of a newspaper. What things would you change to make the format more acceptable and effective.
   March 3 1986
   Dear Editor—I am in complete agreement with your editorial of last Saturday concerning lowering the voting age. The people who disagree with us have not seen both sides of the issue. Best regards,
   William Peters

2. What are the two ways you can underline text in Word-Perfect? Why would you use one method rather than the other?

3. What is the difference between line, page, and print format changes? What is an example of a line format change? a page format change? a print format change?

4. What would the following lines look like on your monitor with the reveal codes removed.

   [Spacing Set:2][C]Welcome to[U]Raquette Lake[u][c][HRt]
   [Tab]Welcome to the beautiful Raquette lake area. We are pleased that you will be our guest.

5. Retype the following title page, bolding the title and underlining the author's name. Save it as a file on your work disk as a file called "title".

   How Automobiles Work
   by
   Richard Exton

6. Go back to the file "title" and retrieve it if it is not already on your screen. Now do the following:
   a) examine the reveal codes
   b) delete the underlining of the author's name
   c) bold the author's name

7. Write out what the reveal codes (or bottom section) of the screen would look like for the following paragraph.

   This is the best convention that I have ever attended. It seems to have everything that the group needs, especially

   adequate rooms
   audio-visual equipment
   nearby restaurants.

   Please send you reservations in before *June 15, 1987*. Thanks from all the people at the Professional Engravers League.

   Be sure to pay attention to *where* the reveal codes should be placed.

8. Type a two-paragraph description of what your day was like yesterday. Be sure to include at least one example of underlining, bolding, and centering of text. When you are finished, print out a copy.

9. Substitute what the reveal codes would look like everywhere there is a "*" for the following paragraph.

    **This is the beginning of a *new* school year. Please try and read *all* the material you have been given by this following Wednesday.

10. What is a default value? When and why would you want to change a default value?

Formatting WordPerfect Lines

After this lesson you'll know

- Why tabs and tab settings are useful.
- How to set single and multiple tabs.
- How to change margin settings.
- When changes in margins can make text more attractive.
- How to change the number of spaces between lines.

Important Terms

aligning characters	margins	tab align
elite	multiple tab feature	tab line
hyphen	pica	tab ruler
left margin	right margin	tab
line format	spacing	windows

Important Keys

Ctrl→End	Ctrl→F6	Shift→F8

In the last lesson, you learned how to make simple format changes like underlining and bolding words. In this lesson, you will concentrate on changing the appearance of WordPerfect lines, such as the margin settings, tabs, and the spacing between lines.

The Line Format Options

To make a change in the format of a WordPerfect line, the Shift→F8 combination of keys is pressed, revealing the **line format** menu you will work with. Make sure that your WordPerfect screen is clear, and then press the Shift→F8 combination of keys. You should see the screen shown in figure 13–1, with the line format menu and its six options across the bottom.

What follows is a discussion of these settings and how each is used to make your WordPerfect documents attractive and effective.

Setting Tabs (Options 1 and 2)

A **tab** is a temporary stop on a line that is activated using the Tab key on your keyboard. Using the tab-setting feature and the tab

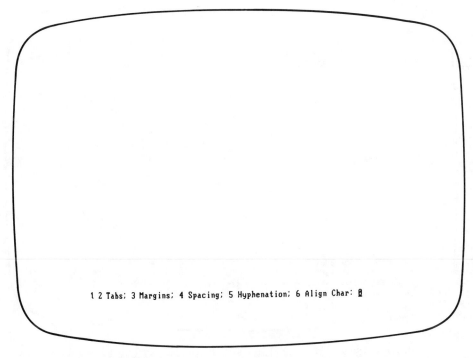

1 2 Tabs; 3 Margins; 4 Spacing; 5 Hyphenation; 6 Align Char: 0

Figure 13–1   Line Format Menu

key, you can move quickly to the same column on different lines. Tab settings and tabs are often used for entering columns of information that need to be aligned. For example, instead of having to use the space bar to move over to column 40 to enter the following set of numbers

                              12
                              22
                              13
                              44
                              28

you can simply set the tab at 40 and move to that position by pressing one key (the Tab key). The tab-setting feature was used to enter the sales information found in figure 8–2.

Select the first or second option from the line format menu. When you do this, your screen should show the line or a set of numbers (which represent spaces on an imaginary line from 1 to 88), as shown in figure 13–2. On the line are *L*s, indicating where tabs are now set. You may notice that the default tab settings are

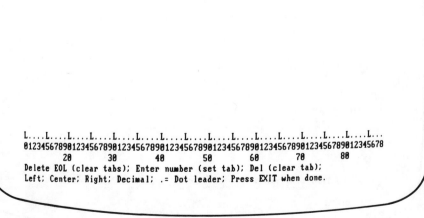

Figure 13–2   Tab Line with Tabs Set Every Five Spaces

5, 10, 15, 20 and so on, by fives up through space 88 on the monitor screen. The line actually extends 270 spaces. You can see the extension beyond your screen's width by pressing the Home→right cursor arrow key, until you get to 270 spaces.

You might not be able to imagine a document that wide, but there are some applications that require very wide **margins**.

To clear the current tab settings and enter a new tab setting at column 50, follow these steps. Be sure that your screen looks like the screen in figure 13–2.

1. Press the Ctrl→End key combination and all the *L*s will be deleted. As you can see in figure 13–3, there are now no active tab settings.

2. Enter the number 50, and press the return key. The number 50 will appear on the screen, and after the return key is pressed, it will disappear. An *L* will appear under the 50 where the tab is now set.

3. Press the F7 key to exit, and the tab is now set at 50. To check the setting, press the Tab key and see how the cursor moves directly to column 50.

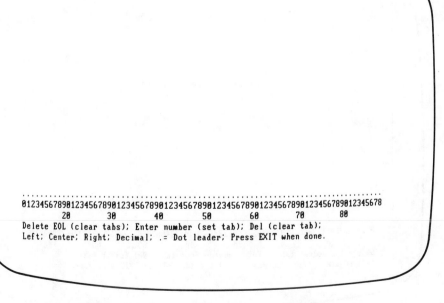

Figure 13–3   Tab Line with No Tabs

Setting Multiple Tabs

If you want to set multiple tabs for stopping at columns 10, 20, 30, and 40 and 50, for example, simply enter each of those values and press the return key each time. From the beginning, and with a clear WordPerfect screen, the sequence of key strokes would be

1. Shift→F8,1

2. Ctrl→End (to clear existing tab settings)

3. 10 <ret>

4. 20 <ret>

5. 30 <ret>

6. 40 <ret>

7. 50 <ret>

8. F7 (to exit)

The tab line shown in figure 13–4 shows these new settings.

Another, more efficient, way to set multiple tabs is to use WordPerfect **multiple tab feature** where you can enter any num-

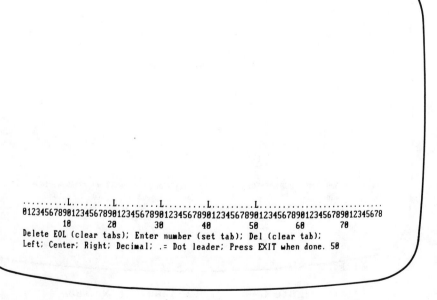

Figure 13–4   Tab Settings at 10, 20, 30, 40, and 50

ber of equally spaced tabs by typing in two numbers separated by a comma. The first number represents the column location of the first tab, and the second number represents the amount of space that is to appear between tabs.

For example, if you want tabs spaced 10 apart beginning in column 0, clear the tab line and enter

0,10 <ret>

If you want tabs spaced 5 spaces apart beginning in column 20, enter

20,5 <ret>

Press the F7 key to enter any changes.

Setting Margins (Option 3)

When you first begin using WordPerfect, the margin settings are 10 spaces from the left side of the screen for the left margin (called the **left margin**), and 74 spaces from the left-hand side of the screen (called the **right margin**) for the right margin. You can change these to any setting you might need, depending on the content of your text and how you might want it displayed.

For example, the Figure 13–5 shows the opening paragraphs of a newsletter article. For a newsletter, the editor needs to reduce margin settings from the more traditional wider line of print. In this case, the editor will use margins of 0 and 30, so the printed final copy looks like a newspaper column.

To change the margin settings, do the following. First clear your screen, and retrieve the file named "news.art".

1. Move the cursor to the first space on the first line of the heading, *Social Events*.

2. Select option 3 on the line format menu (Shift→F8,3). You should now have on your monitor screen the text you typed in, and the following message at the bottom:

[Margin Set] 10 74 to Left =

This tells you that the current margins are set at 10 and 74 and that you are ready to set the new left margin.

3. Enter the number 0 and press the return key. The message line now shows:

[Margin Set] 10 74 to Left = 0 Right =

telling you that the new left margin is 0 and that you are ready to set the new right margin.

```
                   Social Events

       Once again, the executive staff will be challenging the
   different divisions to a softball competition at the annual
   picnic on May 1st at Schrager field (behind the main warehouse
   facility).
       While we know that everyone's insurance is current (the
   company pays for it!), we're all not sure what shape some of last
   year's stars might be in.  So, bring the family, and come out and
   watch.  More details about food and other activities next month.




                                   Doc 1  Pg 1  Ln 1      Pos 10
```

Figure 13–5   Text with Default Margins of 10 and 74

4. Enter the number 30, and press the return. You will see the text with the new margin settings, as shown in figure 13–6.

WordPerfect Hint

Sometimes you need to define margins that are a certain width in inches, rather than spaces. The width in inches depends on the number of printer characters that will fit in one inch. In most cases, there are 10 characters per inch for **pica** *type and 12 characters per inch for* **elite** *type.*

If you need margins at one inch on both sides, the marginal settings for pica are 10 and 75 (since there are 85 spaces on a page of 8 1/2" paper). For elite type, the settings are 12 and 73.

Remember, that once you change the margins on any text, everything that follows that change will appear differently as well. For example, if you go from margins of 10 and 74 to 0 and 30, you will need to change back to 10 and 74.

```
    Social Events

        Once again, SAMI
    executive staff will
    be challenging the
    different divisions
    to a softball
    competition at the
    annual picnic on May
    1st at William's
    field (behind the
    main warehouse
    facility).
        While we know
    that everyone's
    insurance is current
    (the company pays for
    it!), we're all not
    sure what shape some
    of last year's stars
    might be in.  So,
    bring the family, and
    come out and watch.
    More details about
    food and other
    activities next
    month.

                                Doc 1  Pg 1  Ln 52     Pos 10
```

Figure 13–6   Text with Margins of 10 and 30

The editor of this newsletter needs the material in narrow margins, but there are many other reasons for changing margin settings. For example, on the first draft of a term paper, you might want to set the margins fairly narrow (say at 10 and 60), so there is plenty of room for marginal comments and additions.

Seeing Tab and Margin Settings

WordPerfect offers the feature of being able to see both the tab and the marginal settings as you work on a document. Once tabs are set, you can show them on the monitor screen as you enter text.

Using the Shift→F8,1 combination will show you where the tabs are set, but the **tab line** disappears whenever a new setting is entered.

To see what the current tab settings are, follow these steps to use the **tab ruler**.

1. Press the Ctrl→F3,1,23 <ret> sequence of keys. This selects a special WordPerfect feature called **windows**, which will be covered in detail in lesson 14.

The *23* sets the number of lines in the window and allows for the 24th line to be the visual representation of tab settings that you wanted to see (figure 13–7). Each *triangle* represents a tab setting and each of the *brackets* represents a margin setting.

As you can see in figure 13–7, the tabs are set five spaces apart and the margins are set at 10 ({) and 30 (]). To erase the tab ruler, press the Ctrl→F3→1,24 <ret> key combination. Here, the number of lines in the window is increased from 23 to 24, and the tab ruler cannot be seen. The tab ruler is especially helpful when you need to plan out how columns on a page might appear.

Setting Spaces between Lines (Option 4)

Another important formatting feature that almost all word processors offer is the ability to adjust the number of blank lines that occur between lines of text. The number of spaces that you want to appear between lines of text often depends on several factors. Probably the most important is the kind of document you are typing. A letter like the one shown in figure 10–1 is *single spaced* to make

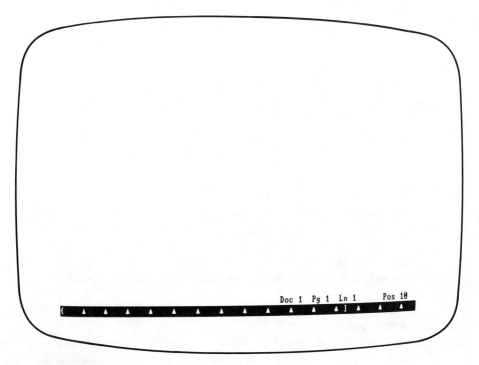

Doc 1 Pg 1 Ln 1   Pos 10

Figure 13–7   The Tab Ruler Showing Margins ({]) and Tab Settings

the text appear "tight" and to the point. Remember, the way that things look can often contribute to their effectiveness. On the other hand, other kinds of documents should be *double spaced*, and, in some cases, *triple spaced*.

For example, a draft of a committee report should be double spaced so there is room for committee members to enter comments. Large manuscripts, such as books or training manuals, should also be double spaced so that *copy editors* can enter their comments and *typesetters* can clearly understand what changes need to be made. As you probably know, it is very difficult to write anything between two lines of text that do not have a space between them.

WordPerfect is set up so there are no spaces between lines of text. In other words, the **spacing** is set at single. To change the setting from 1 blank line between text to another setting, follow these steps. First, clear your screen and recall the file titled "comp.rep".

1. Move your cursor to the top of the report, beginning with the words, *Here are some of the really outstanding. . .*

2. Use the Shift→F8,4 sequence of keys to select the spacing option.

3. The message line on you screen should read

    [Spacing Set] 1

4. Type in the number 2 as the number of spaces that you want between lines of text and press the return key.

The report should now appear double spaced. You can reset the spacing as many times as you want in a document and at any point in the document. For example, quotations are often single spaced in a paper where the text is double spaced. To single space a quotation you have to reset the spacing to single space and then reset it back to double space. Remember, however, that the text below the place you reset the spacing will be changed.

Using Hyphens (Option 5)

The fifth option on the line format menu is hyphenation. A **hyphen** is a grammatical mark that separates syllables in a word. They are used mostly at the end of lines, where there is not enough room for a word to completely fit. Usually, when WordPerfect encounters a word that is too long for a line, it simply moves the entire word to the next line and your document has no hyphens. While this is easy and convenient, you may want to break up

words so that the right-hand edge of the document looks more uniform.

For example, look at these sentences with and without the hyphenation feature.

> This is an entertaining program but very
> instructive. You really do the things that automotive
> engineers do with their much larger and powerful
> computers. Being able to choose from 23 types of engines,
> 6 different types of transmissions and 9 different
> types of brakes lends lots of excitement, potential and
> reality of the design and testing process.

With the hyphenation feature active, the same paragraph
could be rewritten

> This is an entertaining program but very instruct-
> ive. You really do the things that automotive engineers
> do with their much larger and powerful computers. Being
> able to choose from 23 types of engines, 6 different
> types of transmissions and 9 different types of brakes
> lends lots of excitement, potential and reality of the
> design and testing process.

You can see that although only one word (instructive) was hyphenated, the appearance of the entire paragraph is improved.

To use the hyphenation feature follow these steps.

1. Be sure that you have finished typing in the entire document
    that you are working on. The hyphenation feature works best
    when it considers all the text.

2. Move the cursor to the point at which you want the hyphena-
    tion feature to become active, which is usually at the begin-
    ning of the document.

3. Enter the Shift→F8→5,1 sequence of keys which turns on the
    hyphenation feature.

4. Now scroll through the document using the PgDn key. Each
    time you get to a word that WordPerfect thinks could be hy-
    phenated, WordPerfect will stop and give you this message at
    the bottom of the monitor screen

    Position Hyphen; Press ESC

    asking you to use the left and right arrow cursor keys to move
    where you want the hyphen placed, which should be between
    syllables. WordPerfect will only select those words to be hy-
    phenated that appear at the ends of lines.

If you do not know how the word in question is broken down
into syllables, use a dictionary to find out. Once you know where

you want to place the hyphen, press the Esc key, and the selected word will become hyphenated. WordPerfect will continue to select words that you may want to hyphenate. If you do not want to hyphenate a particular word, simply press the F1 function key.

When you are finished with the document, or you no longer want to hyphenate words, turn hyphenation off through the following key sequence: Shift→F8,5,2.

Should you hyphenate? For the most part, it is a personal decision. If you don't, then you cannot misjudge the correct placement of the hyphen between syllables. If you do it correctly though, you are assured of a more uniform looking document.

Aligning Characters

Finally, the last format feature you can take advantage of is **aligning characters** in columns. For example, if you need to type a column of numbers containing a decimal point, as shown in figure 8–2, this option is very useful. The align character feature lines up text vertically on any number, character, or symbol that you select.

The most common use of this feature is when people construct tables and line up decimal points, as was done in Figure 8–2. To use the align feature, follow these steps. Be sure that your WordPerfect screen is clear.

1. Select the align char feature from the line format menu by pressing the Shift→F8,6 sequence.

2. The following message should appear at the bottom of the monitor screen:

    Align Char = .

3. Select the character you want to use for the alignment. As you can see, the default character is the decimal point. Press the F1 key to get back to a clear screen.

4. Whenever the Ctrl→F6 (**Tab Align**) key combination is pressed, the cursor will move to whatever the next tab stop is, and the Align Char = . message will appear again as a reminder.

Now, any text that is typed in will appear to the left of the cursor (with the cursor at the tab set), until the decimal point is typed. For example, to create the two columns of numbers you see in figure 13–8, the Ctrl→F6 keys are pressed until the cursor arrives at the tab stop where the first align character is to be placed (which, in this case, is column 20). Any numbers that are then typed in (12) will appear to the left of the decimal. The decimal

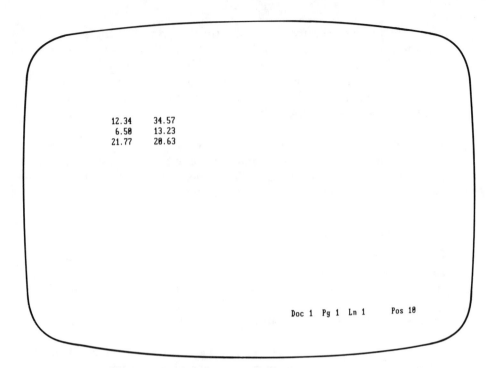

```
      12.34    34.57
       6.58    13.23
      21.77    20.63
```

```
                         Doc 1  Pg 1  Ln 1      Pos 10
```

Figure 13–8   Using the Tab Align Feature at Columns 20
and 30

point (or whatever the designated align character is) is then typed.
Now WordPerfect knows to place the additional characters (34) *after* (and to the right of) the decimal. The Tab key is pressed again
to move over to column 30, where the sequence of keys pressed is
34.57.

You can see how setting things like spacing, margins, and tabs
is simple and straightforward using WordPerfect. Based on what
you learned in lessons 12 and 13, you should now be able to control
many different features of a WordPerfect document. The next lesson finishes the three-lesson set on formatting. Lesson 14 empha-
sizes the appearance of the WordPerfect page and how features
such as page length and page headings can be put to your advantage.

LESSON 13 EXERCISES

1. Write out what the actual tab settings would be for the following WordPerfect tab changes.

    20,20
    5,1,
    12,15
    10,10

2. Type in the following list of numbers, using a multiple tab setting of 0,10.

    1,2,3,4,5
    10,20,30,40,50
    100,200,300,400,500

3. Retrieve the file "news.art" and change the margin settings to 25 and 50 and the spacing to 2.5.

4. What would be the actual margin settings and line spacing, using the following reveal codes, for the following section of text from the "news.art" file?

    [TAB]{Spacing Set:1][Spacing Set:2][Margin Set:12,50] Once
    again, the executive staff will be challenging the different
    divisions to a softball competition at the annual picnic onc
    May 1st at Schrager field (behind the main warehouse
    facility).

5. What margin settings could you use for the following documents? Why?
    a. a newsletter column
    b. a business letter
    c. a term paper
    d. three columns of numbers

6. Type the following paragraph with margins of 10 and 50 and double spaced.

    There's no question that he would be nominated for the
    position of treasurer. He had the experience and the years in
    previous administrative positions, and everyone looked
    forward to his serving.

7. In what situation might you single, double, or triple space a document?

8. Align the following set of numbers into three columns at 12, 24, and 36 column positions.

    1,2,3
    12,23,34
    123,234,345

LESSON 14

Formatting a WordPerfect Page

After this lesson you'll know

- How to chose a position for a page number.
- How to assign a new page number.
- The difference between Arabic and Roman numbering systems.
- When and how to center an entire page from top to bottom.
- That the standard page length is 54 lines and how it can be changed to legal size of 72 lines or customized.
- How to advance to a new page.
- How to set the top margin and change it from the default value of one inch.
- How to use headers and footers on individual pages.
- How to right justify text.
- How to underline in a variety of different styles.

Important Terms

Arabic numerals
continuous single underlining
continuous double underlining
front matter
headers and footers

non-continuous double underlining
non-continuous single underlining
page format
page length
page number position

pagination
print format menu
right justify
Roman numerals
top margin

Important Keys

Alt→F8   Ctrl→F8   Ctrl→N (ˆ)
Ctrl→B (209)

Just as you can format the way a line appears, including such things as its length and spacing, you can also change the format characteristics of an entire page through the use of **page format** options.

The Page Format Options

For page format changes, the combination of the Alt and the F8 keys are used. Clear your WordPerfect screen and press the Alt→F8 key combination, and you will see how WordPerfect offers a variety of options to change the appearance of a page, as shown in figure 14–1.

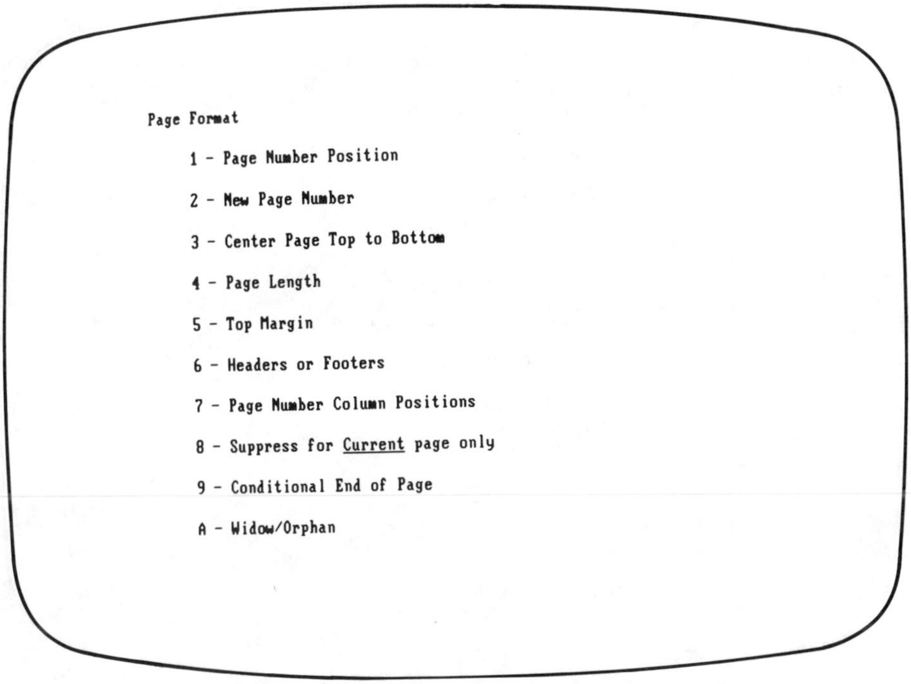

```
Page Format

        1 - Page Number Position

        2 - New Page Number

        3 - Center Page Top to Bottom

        4 - Page Length

        5 - Top Margin

        6 - Headers or Footers

        7 - Page Number Column Positions

        8 - Suppress for Current page only

        9 - Conditional End of Page

        A - Widow/Orphan
```

Figure 14–1   Page Format Menu

What follows is a discussion of the options that you are most likely to be using: numbering pages, assigning a new page number, centering a complete page, changing the page length, setting the top margin, and using headers and footers. You'll also learn in this lesson about special kinds of underlining and justifying (making the right-hand edge of the printed page even).

Numbering Pages

WordPerfect is not preset to assign page numbers to a document. This means that if you want the pages of your document numbered, then you have to select the **page number position** option (option 1), offered on the page format menu shown in figure 14–1.

The complete sequence of keys pressed is Alt→F8,1, which will produce the menu of choices you see in figure 14–2. Clear your WordPerfect screen and press that combination of keys now.

You can see in Figure 14–2 that the choices are straightforward. For example, if you want no page numbers, simply enter a 0. If you want a page number placed at the top right-hand corner of each page, then select option 4. You can even alternate pages, by selecting option 8. In this case, page numbers will alternate

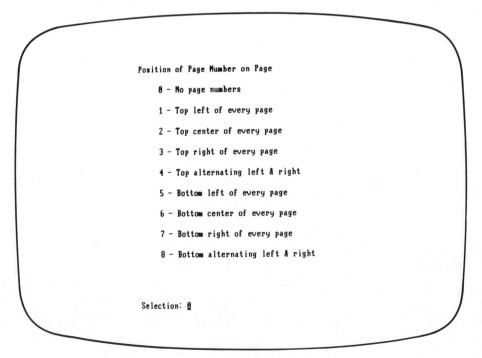

```
Position of Page Number on Page

    0 - No page numbers

    1 - Top left of every page

    2 - Top center of every page

    3 - Top right of every page

    4 - Top alternating left & right

    5 - Bottom left of every page

    6 - Bottom center of every page

    7 - Bottom right of every page

    8 - Bottom alternating left & right



Selection: 0
```

Figure 14–2   Page Number Position Menu

between the left and the right lower corners of the pages in the document. Page numbers are invaluable, especially in a long document. And, if the document is to be read and commented on by others, the page numbers must be there for reference.

Assigning a New Page Number

People often need to change a page number. For example, if there is an extensive amount of **front matter** in a report or a book, the author might want the **pagination** feature to begin on the first page of actual text and to ignore the preface, introduction, or table of contents that usually make up the front matter. To assign a new page number, select option 2 on the page menu shown in figure 14–1.

An author may want to number this front matter using a different numbering system (such as **Roman numerals**), as in this book, and then change to **Arabic numerals** as the text begins. A table of contents for a book with front matter and five chapters using two different numbering systems is shown in figure 14–3.

When you want to assign a new page number, place the cursor on the page where you want the new numbering to begin. Then,

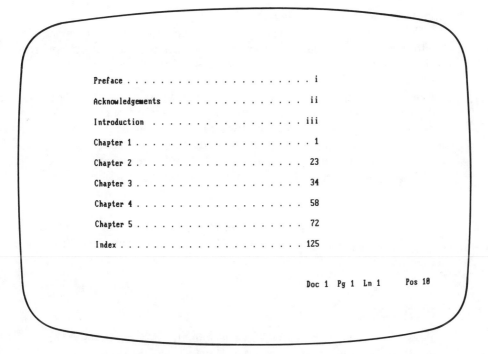

Doc 1 Pg 1 Ln 1   Pos 18

Figure 14–3   Table of Contents

press the Alt→F8,2 sequence of keys, which will produce the prompt

New Page#:

WordPerfect will wait for you to enter the new page number. Once this is entered, WordPerfect will then ask you which of the two choices of number styles you want to select:

Numbering Style Arabic 1; Roman 2: 0

For the table of contents in figure 14–3, the pages of front material use Roman numbers, and the text use Arabic numerals. Remember, that setting a new page number will change only those pages that follow the change, and none of the pages that came earlier.

Centering a Complete Page

In some cases, such as the title page of a report, you may want to *vertically* center the entire page of text. What this means is that there will be an equal space from the *top* of the page to the first line of text and from the last line of text to the *bottom* of the page. If you center each line, as you learned about in lesson 12, and center the page from top to bottom, then the text should appear in the middle of the monitor screen.

Figure 14–4 shows the title page of a company's annual report to stockholders. You can see how the text is centered both by line and by the position on the page. To center an entire page, move the cursor to the top of the page that you want centered and press the following sequence of keys (to select option 3): Alt→F8,3. This tells WordPerfect that all the text on the following page is to be centered. This command must be the first one on the page. You can check this by pressing Alt→F3 and seeing the reveal code.

After the title page is finished, and WordPerfect reaches the next page, the center text option is deactivated automatically.

WordPerfect Hint

Want to see the page you centered on the screen as it will be printed? Use the preview *option (6) from the print menu (Shift→F7) discussed in lesson 6.*

Page Length

Unless WordPerfect receives instructions from you, it sets the **page length** at 54 lines of text. WordPerfect assumes that you are using paper that is 11 inches long, and that each line of type takes

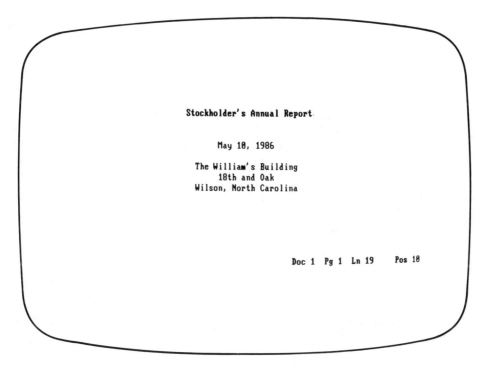

Stockholder's Annual Report

May 10, 1986

The William's Building
18th and Oak
Wilson, North Carolina

Doc 1 Pg 1 Ln 19   Pos 10

Figure 14–4   Centered Title Page

up one-sixth of an inch. You can fit as many as 66 lines of text on
each page.

The main reason why this is not done is because it is not very
neat or readable when there is no top or bottom margin of any
substance. When WordPerfect reaches the end of a page, it automatically goes to the beginning of the next page.

There may be times, however, when you need to change the
length of the page. For example, you might be typing on three-inch
by five-inch index cards. The length of the card is three inches or
18 lines ($3 \times 6 = 18$). Since you want to leave a little space on
each card, the page length should be adjusted to 15, leaving a
small but useful space on the top and bottom of each card.

To change the page length and select option 4 on the page format menu, press these keys: Alt→F8,4. You will be given the
choices shown in figure 14–5. *Option 1,* is the standard letter size,
offering a page length of 66 lines (or 11 inches), and space for 54
lines.

Option 2, is the standard legal size, offering a page length of
84 lines (or 14 inches), and space for 72 lines.

Option 3, is the last option, where you set your own form and

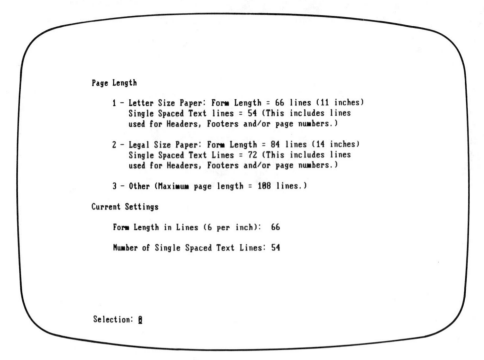

Page Length

    1 - Letter Size Paper: Form Length = 66 lines (11 inches)
        Single Spaced Text lines = 54 (This includes lines
        used for Headers, Footers and/or page numbers.)

    2 - Legal Size Paper: Form Length = 84 lines (14 inches)
        Single Spaced Text Lines = 72 (This includes lines
        used for Headers, Footers and/or page numbers.)

    3 - Other (Maximum page length = 108 lines.)

Current Settings

    Form Length in Lines (6 per inch): 66

    Number of Single Spaced Text Lines: 54

Selection: 0

Figure 14–5   Page Length Menu

text length, with a maximum page length of 108 lines or 18 inches for a maximum number of 96 lines.

Once you make a selection, that is the page length that WordPerfect will use. Since WordPerfect automatically places a one-inch space at the top and bottom of each page (unless told otherwise when you set the top margin, as you will shortly see), you do not need to worry about too many lines of text on any one page. For the most part, the default setting of 54 lines should fit your needs.

Advancing to a New Page: Page Breaks

You may be working on a document and have finished a particular section. It's now time to move on to the next section, but you do not want to begin that next section on the same page. Instead, you want to move to a new page.

This is simple, using the Ctrl→Return combination of keys. WordPerfect will place a double dotted line across the monitor so

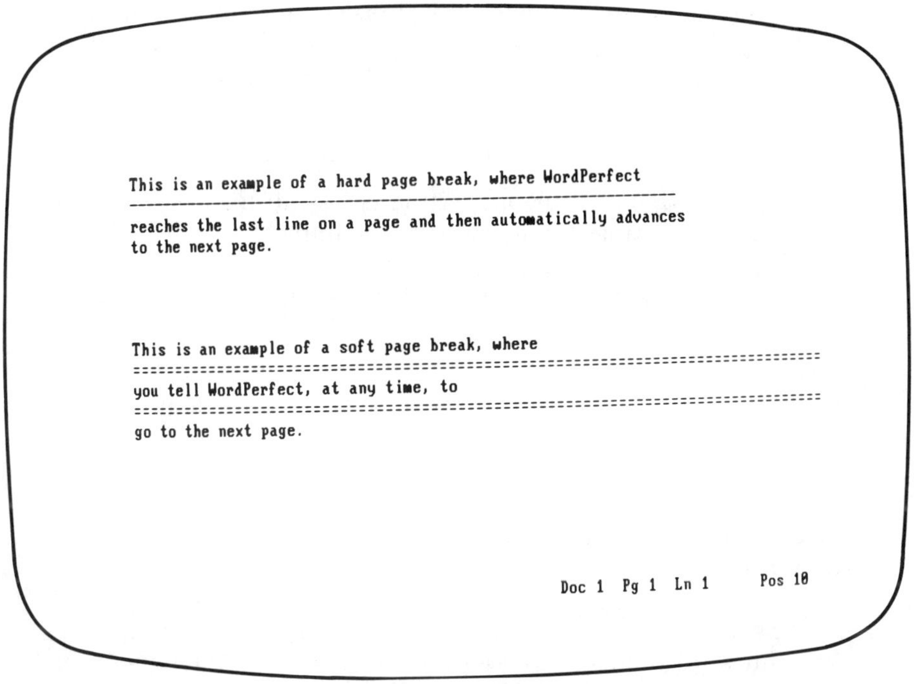

```
This is an example of a hard page break, where WordPerfect
----------------------------------------------------------------
reaches the last line on a page and then automatically advances
to the next page.



This is an example of a soft page break, where
=================================================================================
you tell WordPerfect, at any time, to
=================================================================================
go to the next page.




                                        Doc 1  Pg 1  Ln 1     Pos 10
```

Figure 14–6   Soft and Hard Page Breaks

you can see where the page break is. When printed, WordPerfect will advance to the next page. Anytime you want to advance a page, use this key combination.

WordPerfect Hint	*WordPerfect will automatically insert a page break when the maximum number of lines on a page has been reached. On your screen, as shown in figure 14–6, such a* soft *page break* looks like *a single dotted line. But, when you want WordPerfect to advance to the next page, it shows this* hard page break *as a double dotted line, as shown in figure 14–6*

Top Margin

The **top margin** is the amount of space between the top edge of your paper and the first line of text. As with other WordPerfect page format features, you can adjust this to meet your needs by selecting option 5 from the page format menu.

The preset value for the top margin is one inch or 12 half lines. To change this value, press the Alt→F8,5 sequence of keys. This gives you the following message on the bottom of the monitor screen:

Set half-lines (12→inch) from 12 to

This tells you that the current setting is 12 half-lines or one inch. To change the setting, simply enter in the number of half-lines you want and press the return or enter key.

Here are some margin settings that are already calculated for you.

If you want a top margin of	Enter this many half lines
one-half inch	6
one inch	12
one and one-half inches	18
two inches	24

Why would you want to change the top margin spacing? Perhaps you want to leave room for an illustration on the top of each page or a club or organization logo? Or you only want to print on the bottom half of the page so that other people can add their comments on the top. These are two reasons, but the flexibility of WordPerfect in allowing you to change such things as the size of the top margin is very helpful in producing the kind of appearance you want.

Using Headers and Footers

A nice addition to any printed page is a line of text across the top or the bottom. **Headers** (lines at the top of the page) and **footers** (lines at the bottom of the page) can be used for several things. For example, a header such as Software Report/April Edition might be placed the top of every page of the computer report, as shown in figure 14–7.

Headers and footers can be custom designed to say whatever you want. They can also appear on odd- or even-numbered pages, and on the left or the right of the page. You can have as many as two headers and two footers.

To create a header or a footer, follow these steps.

1. Select the header-footer option (6) using the Alt→F8,6 sequence of keys

```
Software Report/April Edition

                 Software for Children
       Here are some of the really outstanding children's and
   family software that I have come across in the last few months
   during my marketing activities.  We should seriously consider
   making them part of regular offerings to our customers. Most of
   them are reasonably priced, readily available, and may be
   successful items, especially during the holiday sales period.

       Auto Builder gives that budding automotive engineer in the
   family, a chance to design, construct, modify and even test his
   or her own car designs.  This program must be just like the "big
   kids" do in Detroit, only they need to spend thousands of dollars
   rather than $39.95.
       Take your choice and do a station wagon or a sports car, or
   even a new mini-van.  To design a car, you move through certain
   steps beginning with the design of the car's mechanical insides
   including the length of the chassis, gear ratios, tires and more.
   Then you move on to the outside of the car where you get a chance

                                   Doc 1  Pg 1  Ln 43     Pos 10
```

Figure 14–7   Example of a Header

2. You should then see a screen of choices, as shown in figure 14–8.

3. To create the header shown in figure 14–7, option 1 was chosen under *Type*, and, since it is to appear on *every page*, option 1 was chosen under the *occurrence* column. A *type A* header or footer will appear on the left-hand side of the page. A *type B* header or footer will occur on the right-hand side of the page.

4. Once you decide where the header or footer will appear and on what pages, WordPerfect provides a blank screen for the header or footer. As you can see in figure 14–9, the header has been entered.

The last thing you need to do is press the F7 or exit key, as instructed in the bottom left-hand corner of the screen.

Headers and footers can be as long as you need them to be, and a header and footer can appear on the same page. You can also have two headers or two footers appear on the same page. If you do this, be sure that they are short enough so they do not overlap when printed.

When you add a header or a footer, WordPerfect will automat-

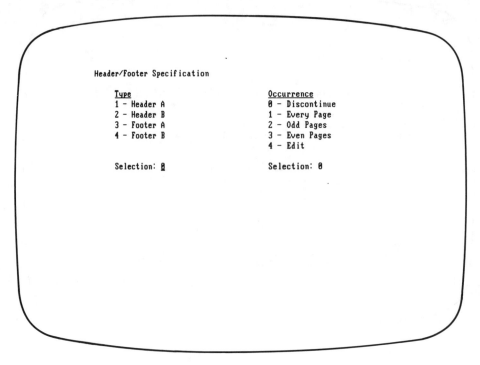

Header/Footer Specification

Type
1 – Header A
2 – Header B
3 – Footer A
4 – Footer B

Occurrence
0 – Discontinue
1 – Every Page
2 – Odd Pages
3 – Even Pages
4 – Edit

Selection: 0

Selection: 0

Figure 14–8   Header/Footer Menu

ically adjust the number of lines on the page so that the header and the footer are included in the total number of lines allowed on the page. For example, on a page with 54 lines, a one-line header leaves room for 53 additional lines.

Editing a Header or Footer

Should you need to edit a header or footer after you have pressed the F7 key, go back to the header- footer menu (shown in figure 14–8), select the type of header you are editing, and select option 4 under the *Occurrence* heading.

WordPerfect will then allow you to edit or re-enter the header or footer.

WordPerfect Hint

Sometimes it's useful to enter the page number as part of a header or footer, so the header or footer includes the current page number. For example, the header on the 27th page of a report might look like this:

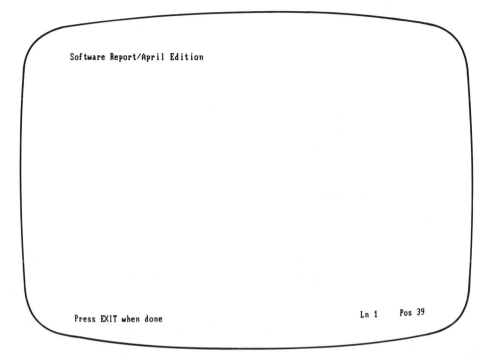

Software Report/April Edition

Press EXIT when done   Ln 1   Pos 39

Figure 14–9   Header/Footer Entry Screen and Header

Car Repair/Chapter 7   Page -27-

To do this, use the Ctrl-B key combination. So instead of the header that was used above being entered as

Car Repair/Chapter 7

it can now be entered as

Car Repair/Chapter 7   Page ^B

Each page will now have the heading, but will also include the page number. The *Page* part of that heading is not a separate header. Spaces were used to separate it from the first part of the header.

Print Format

You've already seen how to change the appearance of lines and pages. Now you'll learn about options that change the way that your documents are printed. Any of the print format options available are illustrated in figure 14–10, which shows the **print format**

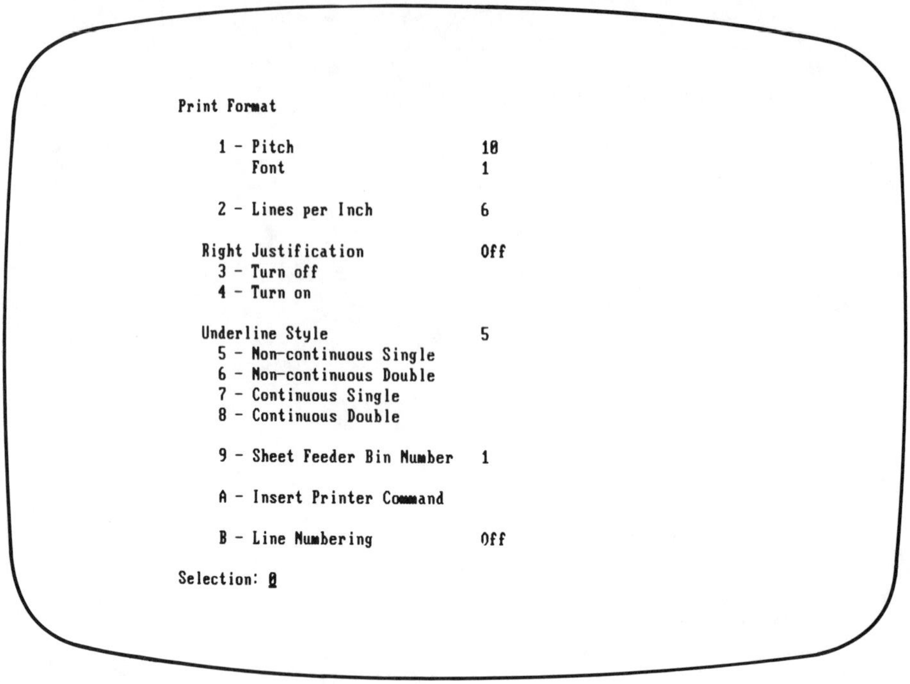

```
Print Format

    1 - Pitch                    10
        Font                     1

    2 - Lines per Inch           6

    Right Justification          Off
    3 - Turn off
    4 - Turn on

    Underline Style              5
    5 - Non-continuous Single
    6 - Non-continuous Double
    7 - Continuous Single
    8 - Continuous Double

    9 - Sheet Feeder Bin Number  1

    A - Insert Printer Command

    B - Line Numbering           Off

Selection: 0
```

Figure 14–10   Print Format Menu

menu. The ones that you will learn about in this part of lesson 14 are right justification and underlining.

Right Justification

A common feature of many word processors is their ability to justify the right-hand edge of the printed text. The left-hand margin of the text is always justified or lined up evenly. When text is right justified, spaces between words are adjusted so that the right-hand edge (as shown below) is even.

> As you can see in this sample of single spaced, right justified text, WordPerfect adjusts the number of words per line and the spacing between them to fit the requirements of right justification.

People feel differently about whether text should be justified or not. You may notice that most textbooks, as is this one, are right justified, and often reports and long documents are done this way to add a more finished appearance to the page. WordPerfect *does not* show right justification on the screen, but will show it when the document is printed or when you preview the document using the preview option on the print menu (Shift→F7,6).

Practice right justifying by first entering the following paragraph and saving under a file name of your choice. Don't forget to clear your WordPerfect screen before you begin.

> One of the managers of the securities division believed that the best investment direction to take involved the selling of certain assets. In particular, holdings in cosmetic and textile industries were sold and the realized capital was reinvested in existing overseas operations.

To activate right justification, follow these steps. Be sure that you have cleared your WordPerfect screen.

1. Move the cursor to the beginning of the place where you want right justification to begin (before the word *One*.)

2. Press this sequence of keys to activate the print format menu, Ctrl→F8,4 and you should see both the menu shown in figure 14–11 and the message that the right justification option is turned on.

3. Press the return key to return to the document you are working on.

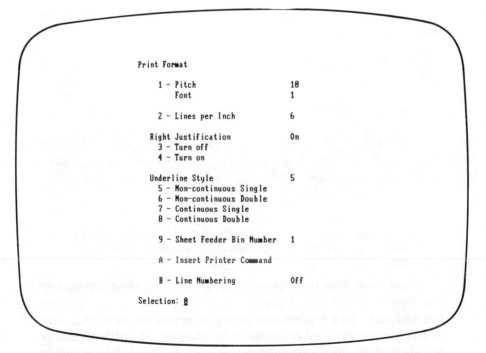

Figure 14–11   Print Format Menu with Right Justification Turned On

4. Move the cursor to the place you want right justification turned off and enter the Ctrl→F8,3 sequence of keys, which turns off the right justification option.

5. Remember, you *cannot* see right justification on the screen. The only way that you can see it is by printing out the document or using the preview option. Now use the Shift→F7,1 key combination and print out the paragraph you just right justified.
    The paragraph will appear as follows:

    > One of the managers of the securities division believed that the best investment direction to take involved the selling of certain assets. In particular, holdings in cosmetic and textile industries were sold and the realized capital was reinvested in existing overseas operations.

Underlining Options

As you learned in lesson 12, underlining a <u>word</u> or even one <u>letter</u> adds emphasis and can be an attractive addition to any text. Using the print format menu, you can underline in a variety of ways besides the continuous single line that you see in the previous sentence.

For example, when you need to underline a set of words, it can appear in one of four ways:

non-continuous single   Call <u>me</u> at <u>ten.</u>
non-continuous double   Call <u>me</u> at <u>ten.</u>
continuous single   <u>Call me at ten.</u>
continuous double   <u>Call me at ten.</u>

Some printers do not have the capability to do double underlining. If yours does not, don't be overly concerned. The single continuous underlining style is adequate and, in many cases, preferred.

To practice the underline feature, return to the paragraph that you just used to practice right justification and follow these steps.

1. Place your cursor at the beginning of the word (or letter) you want to underline. In this case, it is the first word of the first sentence, *One.*

2. Underline the first sentence using the block feature described in lesson 12.

3. Place the cursor at the beginning of the sentence, and use the following keys to select the print format menu and the underlining style *non-continuous single*, which is option 5: Ctrl→F8,5.

4. Check the reveal codes to see that the underline code is entered.

5. Print out the paragraph. It should look like this:

> One of the managers of the securities division believed that
> the best investment direction to take involved the selling of
> certain assets. In particular, holdings in cosmetic and textile
> industries were sold and the realized capital was reinvested in
> existing overseas operations.

As with right justification, WordPerfect does not show the type of underlining on the screen.

LESSON 14 EXERCISES

1. Design the front title page of a term paper where the entire page is centered using the option discussed in this lesson. Be sure to include a title, your name, your school and the date.

2. Type one paragraph on a page and number the page as follows:
    a) The page should be number 11, using an arabic numeral.
    b) The page number should appear in the center of the bottom of the page.

    Print out a copy of the page.

3. Use the header and footer options to produce an *exact* copy of the following page:

    The Civil War   Bill Stone

                              [text]

                            Page -3-

4. Provide an example of three situations where you would want to use both Arabic and Roman numerals. When would you want to have *no* page numbers on your pages and why?

5. The following paragraph is right justified. What's wrong with the appearance? What might be a general rule to help you decide whether to justify text or not?

    This is a cumbersome and significant factor, however, involved in every   facet of the exploration undertaken by the expedition.

6. Underline all the words in the following paragraph with continuous single underlining and print out a copy. Now go back and erase the underline command (use the reveal codes) and then underline using non-continuous style and print out another copy.

    Many people have found that using a word processor such as WordPerfect has made them more efficient in their office and home. They can now write and store letters and other documents for later review and editing.

7. Use the paragraph from exercise 5 and assign the following format settings:
    a) Set the top margin to one-half inch.
    b) Change the length of the page to 30 lines.
    c) Assign a page number of 27.
    d) Have the page number appear in the upper right-hand corner of the page.
        When you are finished with the format settings, print out a copy.

Lesson 15
WordPerfect Windows

After this lesson you'll know.

- What the windows feature of WordPerfect can do for you.
- What a split screen is and how to create it.
- How to work on two files at the same time.
- How to move text material from one document to another when they are each on separate parts of the screen.

Important Terms

split screen   windows

Key Terms

Ctrl→F3   Ctrl→F4   Shift→F3

WordPerfect offers you many different features that make using a word processor easy and efficient. There is one especially useful feature that helps you work on several different documents at the same time! For the person who needs to be editing one document while reading from another, or wants to copy a part of one document to another, WordPerfect has just the thing—**windows!**

The Windows Feature

What the windows feature of WordPerfect allows you to do is to work on *two documents at once*. For example, you might be writing a cover letter to accompany a report. Using the windows feature, you can actually type the letter while viewing any page of the report.

How does WordPerfect do this? It splits your monitor screen into separate parts; in each of these parts, you can see a different file (or document). For example, figure 15–1 shows you a *split screen* with a section of the software report in the upper half and the beginning of a letter in the bottom half. You can see that there are different documents, document 1 and document 2. You already

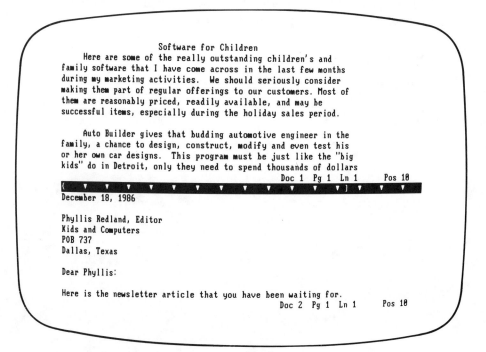

Figure 15–1   Split Screen with Two Documents

know from lesson 14 that WordPerfect allows a total of 24 single spaced lines on a screen. The split screen you see in figure 15–1 has 12 lines in each of the two windows.

To create a window and view two different documents, follow these steps. Be sure that your WordPerfect screen is clear.

1. Retrieve the "comp.rep" file, which is and will be document 1.

2. Press the Ctrl→F3 key combination, and you will see a message line at the bottom of your page as shown in figure 15–2.

3. While there are many other options available on the message line, the one you will work with is option 1, or windows. Select this option. As you can see in figure 15–3, the next message line,

Lines in this Window: 24

will ask you how many lines you want in the window. You can choose from 0 to 24. Enter the number 12 and press the return key. As you can see in figure 15–4, you have split the screen into two equal halves with the upper half filled with part of document 1 and the bottom half blank. You can always tell

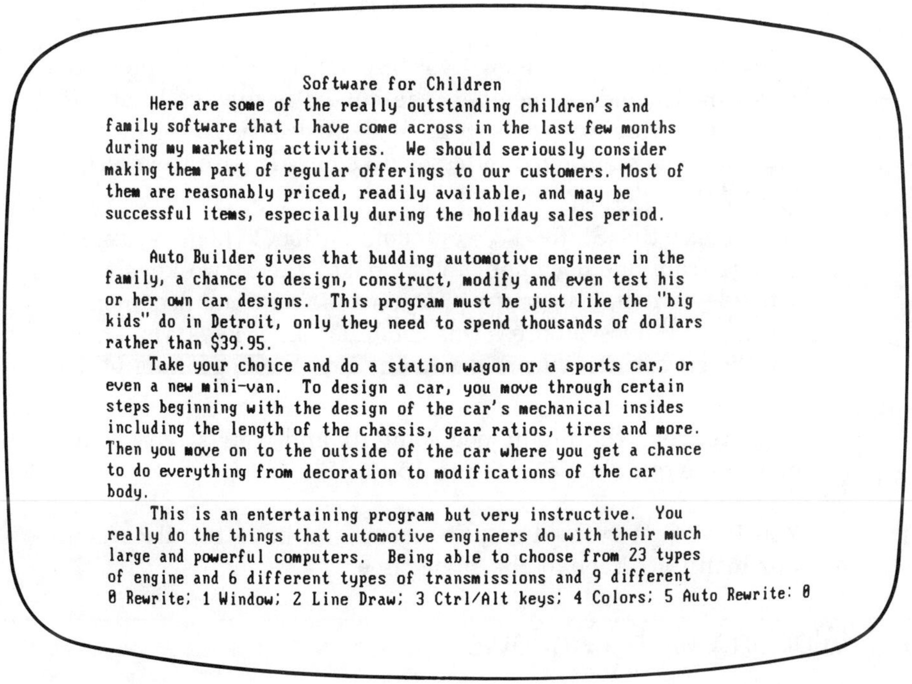

Software for Children

Here are some of the really outstanding children's and family software that I have come across in the last few months during my marketing activities. We should seriously consider making them part of regular offerings to our customers. Most of them are reasonably priced, readily available, and may be successful items, especially during the holiday sales period.

   Auto Builder gives that budding automotive engineer in the family, a chance to design, construct, modify and even test his or her own car designs. This program must be just like the "big kids" do in Detroit, only they need to spend thousands of dollars rather than $39.95.
   Take your choice and do a station wagon or a sports car, or even a new mini-van. To design a car, you move through certain steps beginning with the design of the car's mechanical insides including the length of the chassis, gear ratios, tires and more. Then you move on to the outside of the car where you get a chance to do everything from decoration to modifications of the car body.
   This is an entertaining program but very instructive. You really do the things that automotive engineers do with their much large and powerful computers. Being able to choose from 23 types of engine and 6 different types of transmissions and 9 different
0 Rewrite; 1 Window; 2 Line Draw; 3 Ctrl/Alt keys; 4 Colors; 5 Auto Rewrite; 0

Figure 15–2   Computer Report with Screen Message Line

```
               Software for Children
     Here are some of the really outstanding children's and
  family software that I have come across in the last few months
  during my marketing activities.  We should seriously consider
  making them part of regular offerings to our customers. Most of
  them are reasonably priced, readily available, and may be
  successful items, especially during the holiday sales period.


     Auto Builder gives that budding automotive engineer in the
  family, a chance to design, construct, modify and even test his
  or her own car designs.  This program must be just like the "big
  kids" do in Detroit, only they need to spend thousands of dollars
  rather than $39.95.
     Take your choice and do a station wagon or a sports car, or
  even a new mini-van.  To design a car, you move through certain
  steps beginning with the design of the car's mechanical insides
  including the length of the chassis, gear ratios, tires and more.
  Then you move on to the outside of the car where you get a chance
  to do everything from decoration to modifications of the car
  body.
     This is an entertaining program but very instructive.  You
  really do the things that automotive engineers do with their much
  large and powerful computers.  Being able to choose from 23 types
  of engine and 6 different types of transmissions and 9 different
  # Lines in this Window: 24
```

Figure 15–3   Computer Report with # Message Line

what document (or window) you are working in by where the
cursor is located. Remember, the cursor is always located in
the active window. You can also see in figure 15–4 the *ruler
line* that was mentioned in lesson 13 showing both the margins
({) and the tabs.

4.   Now press the Shift→F3 key combination, which is used to
     change from one document to the next. These two keys act as
     a toggle switch, allowing you to switch from one document to
     the other. When you press this combination of keys, you should
     see the cursor move from document 1 to the beginning of doc-
     ument 2.

5.   Now, retrieve the file named comp.ltr and your screen should
     match the one shown in figure 15–1.

You have just created a split screen and have two documents
on your monitor screen at the same time.

Working with Windows

You can switch between documents at any time and work on one
without affecting the other. They are completely independent of

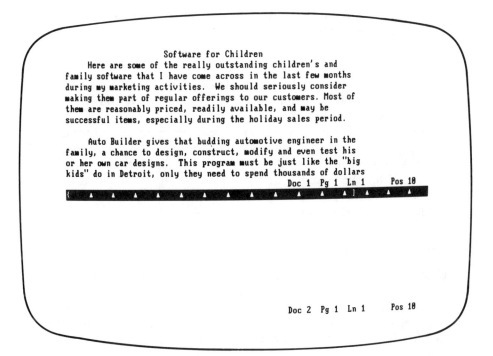

Software for Children
    Here are some of the really outstanding children's and
family software that I have come across in the last few months
during my marketing activities. We should seriously consider
making them part of regular offerings to our customers. Most of
them are reasonably priced, readily available, and may be
successful items, especially during the holiday sales period.

    Auto Builder gives that budding automotive engineer in the
family, a chance to design, construct, modify and even test his
or her own car designs. This program must be just like the "big
kids" do in Detroit, only they need to spend thousands of dollars
                                    Doc 1 Pg 1 Ln 1   Pos 10

                                    Doc 2 Pg 1 Ln 1   Pos 10

Figure 15–4   Split Screen with Bottom Half Blank

each other. Switching is as simple as using the Shift→F3 combination of keys. Try this combination now and see how you are
switched from one document to the other.

You'll also notice that, as you switch documents, the position
of the *tab markers* changes. If you are working on document 1, the
tab markers (little triangles) point up. If you are working on document 2, the tab markers point down.

When you are working in one window, you can treat that document as if it were occupying the entire screen. Anything you
would do to a document using the full screen can be done with a
document showing 12, 6, or even 1 line! Of course, the fewer the
lines that are showing, the more you will have to move the cursor
to see the entire document.

For example, one particularly handy operation is moving text
from one document to another while both are on screen. It's simple
to do by following these steps.

1. Block the text you want to move.

2. Cut and move, or copy and move the text using the Ctrl→F4
    keys.

3. Use the Shift→F3 keys to move to the document where you want to move the text to.

4. Use the Ctrl→F4,5 combination to actually move the material.

WordPerfect stores the section of text to be cut or copied until you want to use it again, no matter if it goes into document 1 or document 2.

Being able to move material from one document to another *and* seeing both documents while you are working can have advantages. You don't need to constantly save one document before you can recall another. And, when you want to insert material from one file to another, you can easily see right where it is going without having to exit one document and recall another.

Ending Windows

Ending a window and returning to only one active document is simple. Just do things in the reverse order. First, place the cursor in the document you want to work on in a full screen. Then, using the Ctrl→F3,1 combination when asked how many lines, enter the number 24 <ret>. You will now have a full screen of the document you want.

LESSON 15 EXERCISES

1. List five examples where using the windows feature of WordPerfect would help make your word processing easier.

   a. _____
   b. _____
   c. _____
   d. _____
   e. _____

2. Enter the following short letter from a friend who is coming to visit.

   Dear Susan,

   It was wonderful seeing you once again, and I was very
   pleased to hear that the project has been so successful. Please
   let me know the exact time that your plane will be arriving
   and I will meet you at the airport.

   Best,

   Carol

   Now, split your monitor screen so that you can write a response to that letter as document 2, telling Carol what time her plane is scheduled to land.

3. What would happen if you created a window with 0 lines? with 24 lines?

4. Clear your WordPerfect screen and recall the file named "comp.rep". do the following:
   a. Create a window for document 2 that has 18 lines.
   b. Move the section in the computer software report on the program named *Auto Builder* from document 1 to document 2. You should now have two windows with text in each one. (Hint: You need to first block the material you are going to move.)

LESSON 16
Checking Your Spelling

After this lesson you'll know

- How to check the spelling of words that WordPerfect recognizes.
- How to check the spelling of words that WordPerfect does not recognize.
- How to correct such mistakes as "double words."
- How to check the spelling of a single word, a page, or an entire document.
- How to add words to your own personal dictionary.

Important Terms

internal dictionary	skip	word count
personal dictionary	spell checker	

Important Keys

Ctrl→F2

Everyone would like to get work done as quickly as possible without making any errors. Unfortunately, the more you rush, the more mistakes you can make and this is certainly the case when entering text. Typing is a wonderful skill to have, but it is one that demands constant practice, and, even then, there are still likely to be *some* spelling errors.

WordPerfect offers you a valuable tool to help you correct any spelling errors you might make. The WordPerfect **spell checker** can check a word, a page, or even an entire document. The spell checker works like this.

WordPerfect has an **internal dictionary.** When you ask it to check your text, it tries to match words in a document with words in the WordPerfect dictionary. If it comes up with a perfect match, it skips that word and goes on to the next word. If it does not come up with a perfect match, WordPerfect will suggest some alternatives. The actual checking process is very quick, and, unless there is a word that WordPerfect does not recognize, the spell checker can zip through a multi-page document in a matter of minutes.

What follows is a step-by-step illustration of how to use the speller. First, be sure that your WordPerfect screen is clear. Now, retrieve the file called "symons.ltr", which should appear on your screen as you see in figure 16–1.

```
March 29, 1986

Ms. Jane Symons
Product Development
Symons Corporation
Chicago, Illinois

Dear Ms. Symons:

Theese are the design plans that we discussed last week at the
the meeting.  They have already been cleared by the various state
and local goverments that will be using the newly designed audio
equipment.

I hope that this is the beginning of our successful prusuit of a
large market share in this area.  Our prelimenary talks have all
pointed towards that goal.


Sincerely,


William P. Moore
Director
Research and Development

                                    Doc 1  Pg 1  Ln 31    Pos 10
```

Figure 16–1   Letter for Spell Check

Starting The Speller

The key combination that begins the WordPerfect speller is Ctrl→F2. Press this combination and your screen should now show the *spell check menu* underneath the symons letter, as shown in figure 16–2.

Before you actually begin using the speller, it is important to understand what each of the six options on the message line does.

1. This option will check the correct spelling of any one *word* that you place the cursor on before you press the Ctrl→F2 combination.

2. This option will check the correct spelling of the words on the *page* that you are currently on when you activate the speller.

3. This option will check the spelling of all the words in an entire *document.*

4. and 5.   are used when you want to create your own dictionary, which only works with the full version of WordPerfect and not the training version.

6. This option will count the number of words in the document and give you a total count. This is a very handy feature, espe-

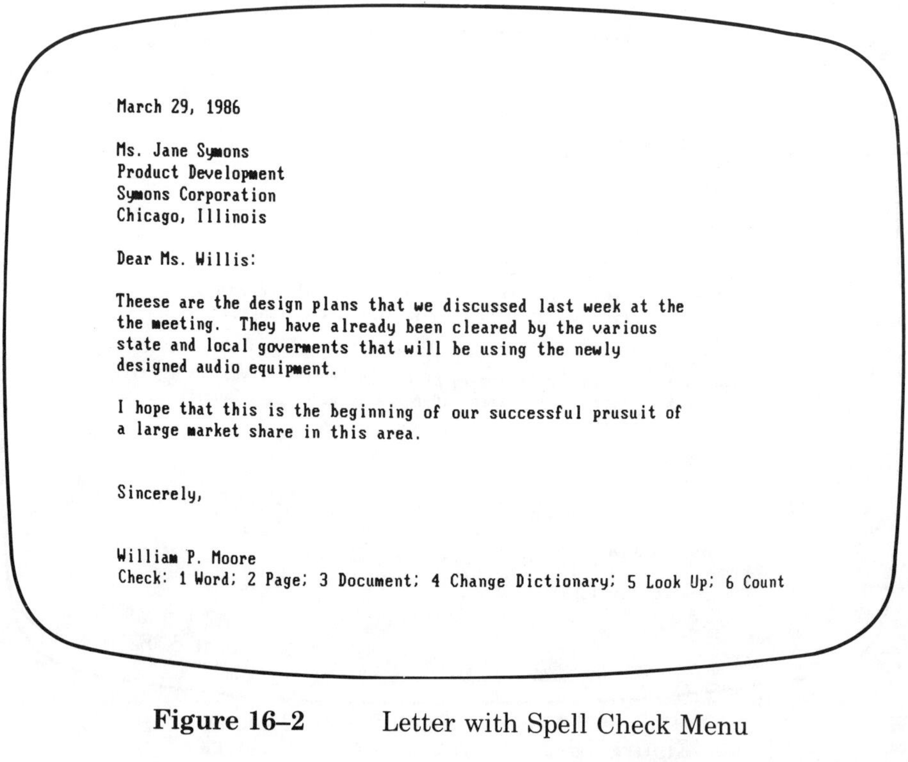

```
March 29, 1986

Ms. Jane Symons
Product Development
Symons Corporation
Chicago, Illinois

Dear Ms. Willis:

Theese are the design plans that we discussed last week at the
the meeting.  They have already been cleared by the various
state and local goverments that will be using the newly
designed audio equipment.

I hope that this is the beginning of our successful prusuit of
a large market share in this area.


Sincerely,


William P. Moore
Check: 1 Word; 2 Page; 3 Document; 4 Change Dictionary; 5 Look Up; 6 Count
```

Figure 16–2   Letter with Spell Check Menu

cially if you are required to meet a certain minimum number of words or not to exceed some maximum.

Using the Speller

Most of the time, you will be interested in checking the spelling in the entire document. With the letter to Ms. Symons on the screen,

---

WordPerfect Hint

Typing or spelling error????? WordPerfect knows to check the words that it does not recognize. There may be words, however, that are spelled *correctly, but* typed *incorrectly. WordPerfect will not know that these need to be corrected.*

FOR EXAMPLE, THE first three words in this sentence are typed incorrectly, since only the first letter of the first word should be capitalized. The correction is not a spelling matter, but an inaccuracy in the typing. WordPerfect will not correct typing errors! It's for this reason that you should not consider the spell checker to be a check on your typing accuracy as much as a checker of misspelled words.

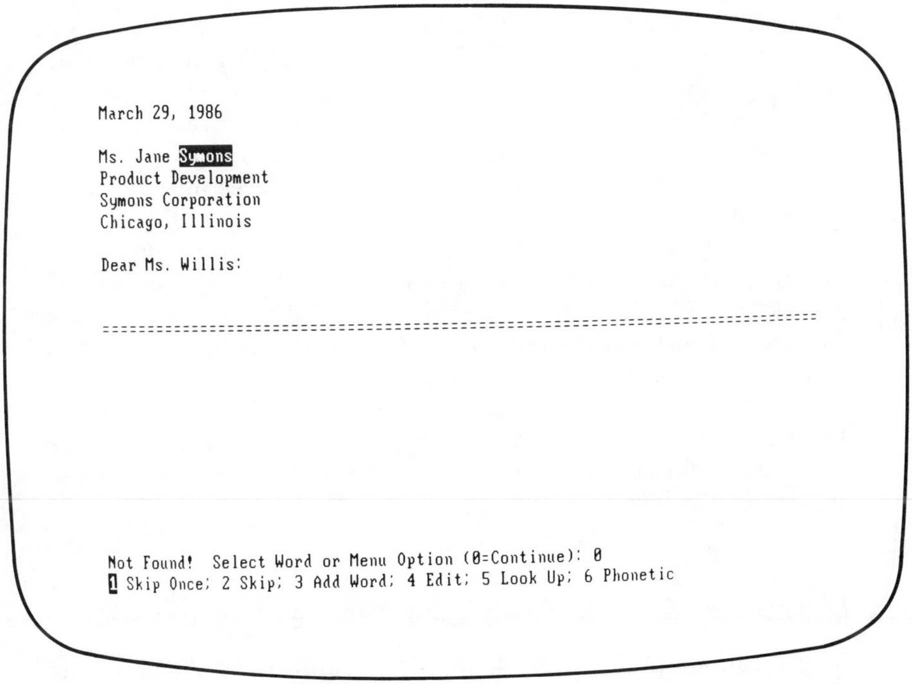

```
March 29, 1986

Ms. Jane Symons
Product Development
Symons Corporation
Chicago, Illinois

Dear Ms. Willis:

=====================================================================================


Not Found!  Select Word or Menu Option (0=Continue): 0
1 Skip Once; 2 Skip; 3 Add Word; 4 Edit; 5 Look Up; 6 Phonetic
```

Figure 16–3   Spell Check Options

select the option (3) that will check the spelling of the entire document. Do that now.

Figure 16–3 shows you what the next monitor screen will look like and the several choices that you now have. The WordPerfect speller will now go through and check each word in the document. When it finds a word it does not recognize, it will ask you to press a key that corresponds to one of the six options listed in the message line at the bottom of the screen.

The options shown in figure 16–3 allow you to skip a word once (option 1), skip every occurrence of the word throughout the document (option 2), add a word to your personal WordPerfect dictionary (option 3), edit a word (option 4), look up the word (option 5), and help find the spelling through the sound of the word (option 6).

Checking Words That WordPerfect Doesn't Know

The first word that the speller stops at is *Jane.* As you might expect, WordPerfect cannot contain *all* the words in the English language in its speller (neither can any other word processing program). Consequently, there will always be some words that it does not recognize. These are words that *you,* and not WordPerfect, will have to decide about.

You probably recognize that *Jane* is spelled correctly, so the proper option to press is 2, **Skip.** This tells WordPerfect not to correct this word, and also skip any more occurrences of it (a great time saver).

You may notice that option 1 only skips this word once. You might want to use this option if you are not sure you spelled a word the same way throughout your document. This is because the WordPerfect speller will only check for a word spelled the way it was when WordPerfect first encountered it.

The next word that the speller stops on is *Symons,* another one to skip (option 2 again). WordPerfect now automatically goes on with its checking, and finds a word *(theese)* that it recognizes as incorrectly spelled.

Checking Words That WordPerfect Knows

As you can see in figure 16–4, WordPerfect offers an alternative to the misspelling. By pressing the letter A, the correct spelling, *these,* is substituted for the wrong spelling, *theese.* WordPerfect

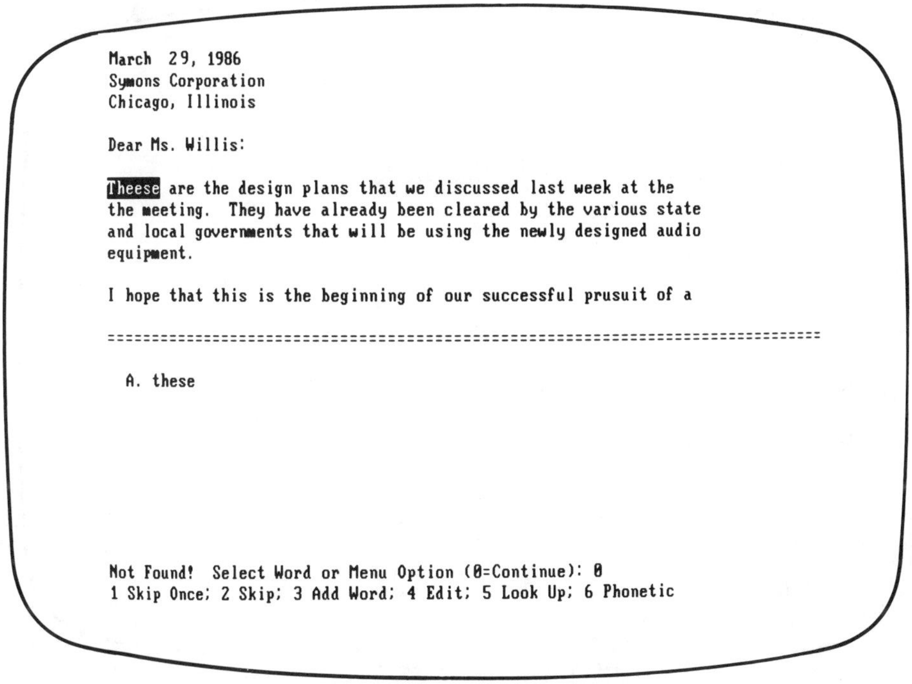

```
March 29, 1986
Symons Corporation
Chicago, Illinois

Dear Ms. Willis:

Theese are the design plans that we discussed last week at the
the meeting.  They have already been cleared by the various state
and local governments that will be using the newly designed audio
equipment.

I hope that this is the beginning of our successful prusuit of a

==================================================================================

  A. these




Not Found!  Select Word or Menu Option (0=Continue): 0
1 Skip Once; 2 Skip; 3 Add Word; 4 Edit; 5 Look Up; 6 Phonetic
```

Figure 16–4   Correction of "theese"

makes the correction in the text, and then moves on to the next
word.

Correcting Double Occurrences

The next occurrence of an error is the double word *the the,* which
WordPerfect can correct when you press option 3 (Delete 2nd).
Here, WordPerfect deletes the second *the.* The WordPerfect speller
will continue to check words until they are all corrected by
WordPerfect, corrected by you, or skipped by you.

Correcting Misspelled Words

As you can see in figure 16–5, the speller stops at the word *prelimenary,* and, after searching in the main dictionary, WordPerfect
turns to you for the next step.

You could press 1 or 2, but you may be skipping a word that is
not spelled correctly (as is the case here). After going to your own
book *dictionary* (if necessary), you find that the word should be
spelled *preliminary.* You should select option 4, *edit,* which allows
you to change the word on the screen.

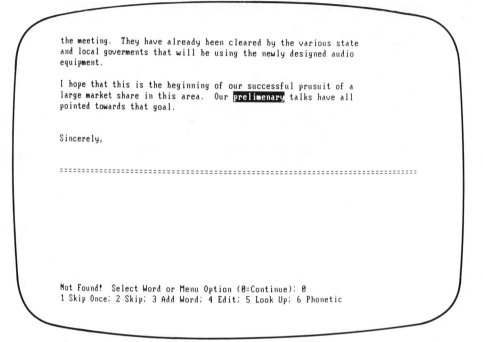

the meeting. They have already been cleared by the various state
and local goverments that will be using the newly designed audio
equipment.

I hope that this is the beginning of our successful prusuit of a
large market share in this area. Our `prelimenary` talks have all
pointed towards that goal.

Sincerely,

==

Not Found! Select Word or Menu Option (0=Continue): 0
1 Skip Once; 2 Skip; 3 Add Word; 4 Edit; 5 Look Up; 6 Phonetic

Figure 16–5   Correction of "prelimenary"

To edit, use the *del* key to erase letters. Then insert the correct spelling. When you are finished, press the *2* (Skip) key, since WordPerfect still does not recognize the word as being spelled correctly or incorrectly.

WordPerfect Hint

Option 4 (edit) can be used to correct any kind of error, be it a misspelling or a run on, *such as* inthis. *Use this option whenever you need to customize a correction. The only thing that you need to remember about using this option to make corrections is that you can only do it on the same line where WordPerfect originally stopped.*

Creating Your Own Dictionary

Another option is what to do when you encounter a word you would like to add to your **personal dictionary.** For example, if you write letters frequently, perhaps you would like to select option 3 and add your name to the dictionary, rather than have WordPerfect stop and ask you what to do each time it does not recognize your

name. Each time WordPerfect encounters your name in *future* letters, it will know how to spell the name, skip it if it is spelled
correctly, or correct it if necessary.

Counting Words

Finally, when WordPerfect is finished checking the spelling, it will
give you a **word count** of the number of words in the document
that is being checked. In figure 16–6, the number of words is *83*,
as you can see by the word count in the lower left-hand corner of
the screen. You can also get a word count by selecting option 6
from the first message line you encountered after you activated the
speller.

WordPerfect Hint	*If you find that in the middle of a document check you need to stop the spell checker, press the F1 key and you will be returned to the active document.*

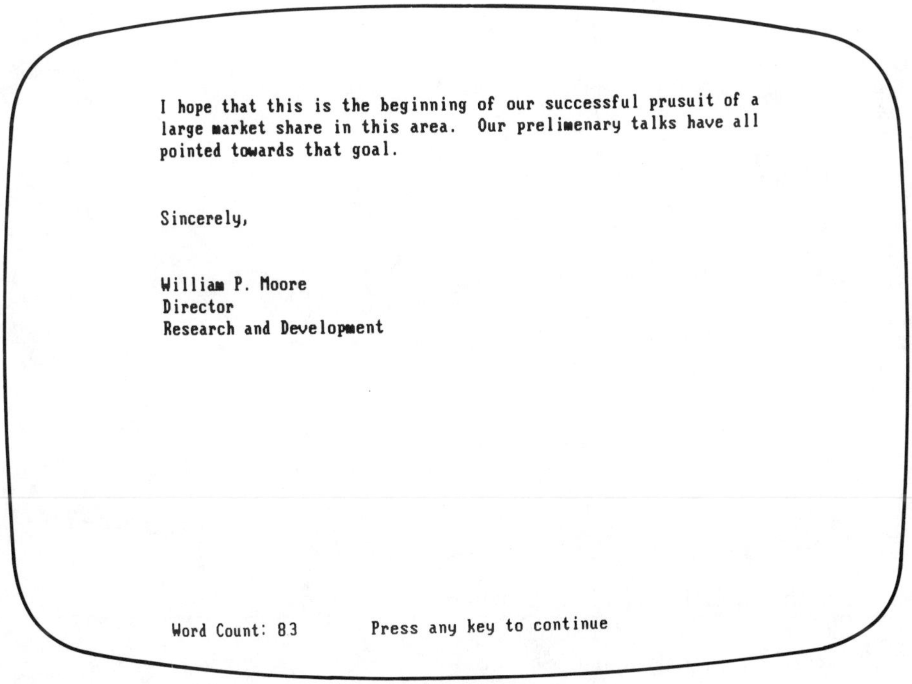

I hope that this is the beginning of our successful prusuit of a
large market share in this area. Our prelimenary talks have all
pointed towards that goal.

Sincerely,

William P. Moore
Director
Research and Development

Word Count: 83   Press any key to continue

Figure 16–6   Spell Check Word Count

Probably the best reason to use the word count is that certain documents need to be limited to a certain number of words. For example, a summary of a report may need to be between 300 and 400 words. This word count tool can be a great help because it can be used as many times as necessary throughout the preparation of a document.

Once the spelling check is completed, you can press any key to return to your active document.

LESSON 16 EXERCISES

1. Below is an announcement of a new course that will be offered at your school next year. It contains five spelling errors. Identify each one, and choose one of the six spell check options shown in figure 16–3 to correct the error.

    Business 102: Dataa Analysis
         This course will offer an introductionto the basic
    principles of data analysis. There are no prequisites, but all
    students should bee familiar with the use of micocomputers.

2. Your WordPerfect spell checker has just stopped at a unique word in a document that you know is spelled correctly. How do you decide whether to add it to your personal dictionary? In general, what types of words should be added to your personal dictionary? What factors contribute to such a decision?

3. While running the spell checker, WordPerfect stops on the following line:

        It was a very strang invitation, to a PARTY. . .

    After you correct *strang* to *strange,* you notice that there is another error on the line that WordPerfect will not recognize. How do you correct it while using the spell checker?

4. Provide three examples where the word count feature of WordPerfect would be useful. How would you use WordPerfect to count the number of words in this paragraph?

5. What is a synonym and why must you be particularly careful after using the WordPerfect spell checker to *read* the document over, even when all the spelling errors are corrected?

6. Count the number of words in the file "comp.rep".

LESSON 17
Doing Outlines

After this lesson you'll know;

- Why outlines are important.
- How an outline can be used as an organizational tool.
- How an outline can be used as a summary tool.
- The number of levels and types of headings the WordPerfect outlining feature offers.
- How to do an outline using WordPerfect.

Important Terms

headings   levels   outline

Important Keys

Alt→F5   Tab

The Use of Outlines in Word Processing

Before people begin writing, they often like to write down their main thoughts to organize the general order in which things will be discussed. They can then see if certain important points may have been left out or how the repositioning of other ideas might help make the finished document clearer. Probably the best available tool to accomplish these purposes is the **outline** feature of WordPerfect.

What is an Outline?

An outline is like the table of contents of a book. It is a set of statements presented in logical order that summarizes a much longer document. These statements are usually organized into sets of major and minor points. For example, figure 17–1 is a brief outline of pointers on writing an effective letter. You can see how there are general headings in the outline (e.g., *What is a good let-*

```
I. What is a good letter?

    A. accomplishes goal
    B. gets job done efficiently
    C. relatively inexpensive
    D. generates "paper trail"

II. Parts of a letter

    A. Introduction

        1. brief and to the point
        2. states purpose of letter

    B. Body

        1. mentions alternatives
        2. focuses on main issues
        3. provides solutions

    C. End

        1. thanks correspondent
        2. proposes next step
        3. salutation

                    Doc 1  Pg 1  Ln 53      Pos 10
```

Figure 17–1   Outline: The Components of a Good Letter

ter? and *Parts of a letter)* and under each of these major headings, additional points are made.

This particular example of an outline has two main headings, but there is no reason why an outline cannot have three, four, or even fifty! In fact, there is no limit to the number of headings an outline can have.

When to Use an Outline

Outlines are usually used in two situations. The first, is when an outline is used *before* the actual writing begins. Here, you may sit down and list all your thoughts and then go back and organize them in the order you think they should appear. When used in this way, an outline becomes an *organizational tool.* It will probably change as you find different ways to organize the material you are writing about.

The second way to use an outline is as a *summary tool,* completed *after* the writing is finished. Here, the outline summarizes the important points of a longer document. This might be particulary helpful if, for example, you need to summarize a long written document.

How an Outline is Organized

Outlines are organized by different *levels,* beginning with the most general level presented first, followed by the next level, and so on. Each level has a unique heading. For example, in the outline shown in figure 17–1, the first level heading uses the roman numeral I and contains information about what makes a good letter. Listed under that heading (using capital letters) are the four points under that major heading. Under the second major heading *(Parts of a letter)*, there is another second level heading *(Introduction)*, but there is an additional level as well, which uses arabic numerals (such as entry II.A.1., *brief and to the point)*.

WordPerfect allows you to have an outline up to *seven* levels deep under any one major heading, with each level represented by a different symbol. These seven levels are shown in figure 17–2.

Figure 17–3 shows the **headings** for a hypothetical outline

I. First level (upper-case Roman numeral)
  A. Second level (upper-case letter)
    1. Third level (Arabic numeral)
      a. Fourth level (lower-case letter)
        (1) Fifth level (lower-case letter with parentheses)
          (a) Sixth level (lower-case letter with parentheses)
            (i) Seventh level (lower-case Roman numeral with parentheses)

Figure 17–2   The Seven Levels of an Outline

I.
   A.
   B.
   C.
II.
   A.
      1.
      2.
III.
   A.
   B.
      1.
      2.
         a.
         b.
         c.
         d.
         e.
IV.
V.
   A.
   B.
   C.
   D.
      1.
   E.
   F.
      1.
      2.
      3.
      4.

Figure 17–3   Three-Level Outline

that has five main headings with various numbers of second-, third-, and fourth-level headings.

Notice how each heading is indented a certain amount of space. This is so that similar levels of information across topics are placed consistently throughout the outline. For example, all second level headings beginning with upper-case letters are indented five spaces from the left-hand margin.

Doing a WordPerfect Outline

Follow these steps to complete a three-level outline that focuses on how to organize and begin a political campaign. Be sure that your WordPerfect screen is clear.

1. Type in, and center the outline title, Beginning a Political Campaign. Press the return key twice.

2. The key combination for doing an outline is Alt→F5,1. This will place you in the outline mode. Press these keys and you should see the word Outline in the lower left-hand corner of your screen.

3. Press the return key once. As you can see in figure 17–4,

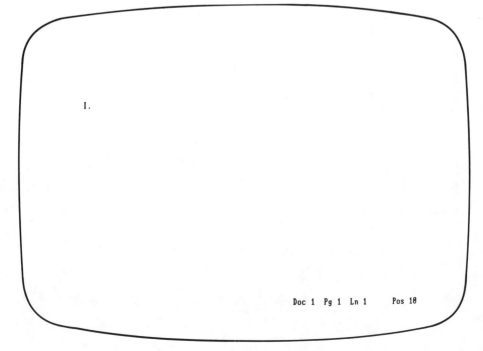

I.

Doc 1 Pg 1 Ln 1   Pos 10

Figure 17–4   Beginning a Political Career

WordPerfect automatically inserts the first level of the outline as I.

Now type in the following after the I. Do not press the return key after you finish typing in this main heading: **Organizing the effort.**

When you do press the return key, you will get a new main heading, II. You now have to decide whether you want to begin at a new main level or press the Tab key, which will give you the *second-level* heading under heading I. The second-level heading is A. The general rule is that when you need to go to a new first-level heading (e.g., II, III, IV, etc.), you press the Return key. The level within any heading that you go to depends upon how many times you press the Tab key. If you don't press the tab key at all, you remain at the first level (I., II., III., etc.). If you press it once, you go to the second level (A., B., C., etc.).

4. Press the Tab key *once,* and enter the second level heading (A) under the first level heading (I), so your outline looks like figure 17–5.

5. Press the return, and tab again until you get to B, and type in

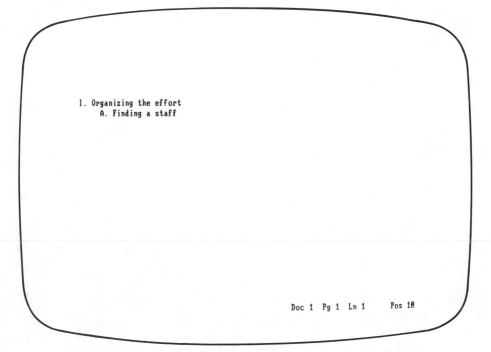

```
I. Organizing the effort
   A. Finding a staff




                                    Doc 1  Pg 1  Ln 1     Pos 10
```

Figure 17-5   Beginning a Political Career, continued

Looking for volunteers. The outline should appear as it does in figure 17–6.

WordPerfect Hint

If you need to make a correction during an outline, have no fear. You can delete any level heading by using the delete and the back space keys. WordPerfect will remember what level was erased, so that the next one that begins in that spot will be in the correct sequence at the same level.

6. Begin a new level and type in *students, retirees,* and *other volunteers,* so the outline, which now has *three* levels, should appear as in figure 17–7. This is a three-level outline with level values that were automatically generated by WordPerfect.

Outlining is a fun and useful tool. You'll find that it can

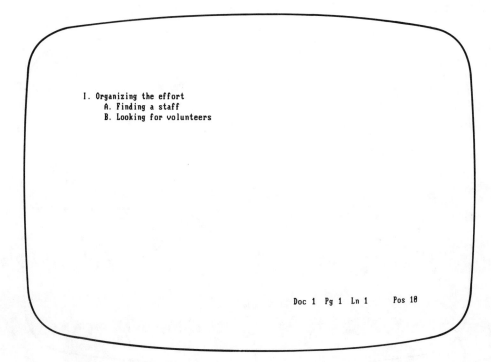

```
I. Organizing the effort
   A. Finding a staff
   B. Looking for volunteers




                                        Doc 1  Pg 1  Ln 1      Pos 10
```

Figure 17–6   Beginning a Political Career, continued

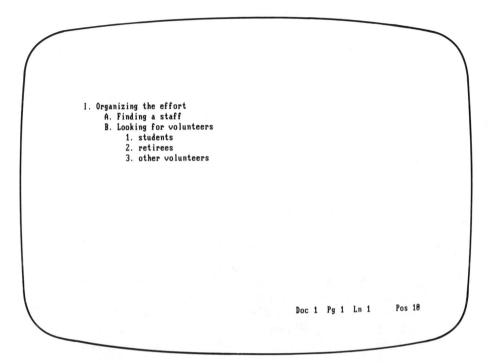

```
I. Organizing the effort
   A. Finding a staff
   B. Looking for volunteers
      1. students
      2. retirees
      3. other volunteers




                                    Doc 1  Pg 1  Ln 1        Pos 10
```

Figure 17–7   Beginning a Political Career, continued

not only help you organize your thoughts before you begin writing, but it can also help you summarize them when you are finished. Almost every successful writer works from some kind of an outline, and with WordPerfect's outlining feature, you get the assistance you need.

LESSON 17 EXERCISES

1. Here is a blank form for a three-level outline. Choose any topic and complete the outline.

   I.
   - A.
   - B.

   II.
   - A.
   - B.
     1.
     2.

2. Name five school assignments that you completed this past semester that you could have used the WordPerfect outlining feature on. How would this have helped your work?

3. Here is an outline of a talk on preparing a dinner party for 12 people. They are in the order in which they should be presented in outline form, but there is no distinction by levels. Use these headings and WordPerfect's outline feature to complete the outline following the model in figure 17–1. In this exercise, you have to decide which information belongs at which levels.

   Invitations
   Deciding on guest list
   Picking cards
   Sending them out
   When?
   Preparation for the party
   The menu
   The first course
   The second course
   The third course
   The fourth course
   Dessert
   Shopping
   Where?
   Final things to remember
   Buy flowers
   Polish silver
   Take tablecloth and napkins to cleaner

LESSON 18
Using Macros

After this lesson you'll know;

- What a macro is.
- Some of the things a macro can be used for.
- How a macro is defined.
- How to begin and design a macro.
- How to repeat a macro any number of times.

Important Terms

esc   macro

Important Keys

Alt→F10   Ctrl→F10

As your word processing skills become more advanced, you will come across situations where you will want to change a part of a letter or a report in a way that goes beyond the simple search and change you learned about in lesson 11. For example, you may be writing several letters and you would like to have your salutation (*Sincerely,* etc.) printed at the end of each one. You could, of course, type the complete salutation each time at the end of each letter. Or, you could use a WordPerfect **macro,** which is a set of keystrokes stored as a separate file and activated by the touch of a few keys. Here, you can have WordPerfect perform any number of steps. And, once macros are defined, they can be saved and retrieved like any other file.

Just think what you could do with macros! You could

- type the standard closing to a letter

- enter all the format commands for a document, such as the margin and spacing settings, headers, and page length

- locate and underline a word that occurs many different times in a document

Defining a Macro

The first step in creating and using a macro is defining it or giving it a name. To do that, you must first indicate that you want to use the macro feature. This is done by pressing the Ctrl→F10 key combination, which gives you the

Define Macro:

message in the bottom left-hand corner of your screen. WordPerfect is asking for the name of the macro you want to assign.

WordPerfect Hint

Keep in mind that naming a macro is just like naming a file. Don't use a name that has no meaning. For example if you are entering a set of keystrokes that provide the salutation to a letter, name it "bye" or "salut", not "macro1" or "macro2".

In the example here, the macro is being named "bye" (for *good-bye).* This is the name that will be used to recall the keystrokes that make up the macro. Once the return key is pressed, the message line becomes a blinking

Macro Def

WordPerfect is asking you to enter the keystrokes that make up the macro "bye".

The complete set of keystrokes for a macro that provides a salutation and a name (use your actual name) is as follows. Be sure that your WordPerfect screen is clear and follow these steps.

1. press Ctrl→F10
2. enter the macro name bye <ret>
3. begin to define the macro by entering Sincerely, <ret>
4. press the <ret> key to enter a space
5. <ret>
6. <ret>
7. <ret>
8. enter your actual name <ret>
9. press Ctrl→F10 to end the macro

These nine steps will be stored under the name "bye". When the macro is activated, the salutation will look like this:

Sincerely,

"Your Name"

Notice that step 8 finishes the macro. When you press the Ctrl→F10 combination a second time, the macro is closed and stored under the name you gave it.

Starting a Macro

Once you have created a macro, starting it is as easy as pressing the Alt→F10 combination. After this, WordPerfect will ask you the name of the macro. Once you type in the name of the macro and press the return key, the macro will automatically begin. In this example, the salutation should appear on your screen.

Be sure that your WordPerfect screen is clear. The keystrokes that begin the macro defined as "bye" are:

1. Alt→F10
2. bye <ret>

Try these steps now and you should see the salutation that you created and stored as a macro. You can now use this macro to automatically type the ending for all of your letters.

Repeating A Macro

Often, you may want to *invoke* a macro more than once. That is, within your letter or report, you need to repeat something several times. The key to making a macro repeat is using the **esc** key, which will give you the message

n = 8

Here, you enter the number of times you want the macro to operate. The number *8* is the default, or the number of times WordPerfect will execute the macro if not told otherwise. In the above example, you only added a salutation *once*.

In the following example, you will see how to repeat a macro three times. Use this paragraph to practice repeating macros. Enter it after you have cleared your WordPerfect Screen.

> WordPerfect is a word processing program that is easy to learn and use. WordPerfect offers many advanced features, but WordPerfect can also be used by the beginner.

The macro you will now enter is designed to find the word *WordPerfect* (which occurs three times) and underline it. When you are finished, the new paragraph will look like this.

> <u>WordPerfect</u> is a word processing program that is easy to learn and use. <u>WordPerfect</u> offers many advanced features, but <u>WordPerfect</u> can also be used by the beginner.

Keep in mind that when you define a macro, you must define it working with actual text. You cannot simply list a series of strokes at the beginning of a blank page. Since these strokes would have nothing to "act on," the macro could never learn what it is supposed to do.

Move to the beginning of the paragraph that you just entered and follow these steps.

1. Ctrl→F10
2. uwp <ret>
3. F2
4. WordPerfect
5. F2
6. Ctrl→Left cursor arrow
7. Alt→F4
8. Ctrl→Right cursor arrow
9. F8
10. Ctrl→F10

11. esc
12. 2
13. Alt→F10
14. uwp
15. <ret>

Here is a description of what each step does.

- Step 1 turns on the macro feature
- Step 2 names the macro "uwp" for *underline WordPerfect*
- Step 3 begins the search feature
- Step 4 tells WordPerfect to search for the word *WordPerfect.*
- Step 5 ends the search function
- Step 6 moves the cursor to the first letter of the word *WordPerfect.*
- Step 7 begins the block function
- Step 8 blocks the word *WordPerfect*
- Step 9 underlines the blocked word
- Step 10 ends the macro
- Step 11 starts the multiple macro function
- Step 12 defines the number of times the macro should be repeated
- Step 13 recalls the macro
- Step 14 names the macro to be recalled
- Step 15 begins the macro

You can design macros to do any number of keystrokes that you need. For example, here's someone's stationery heading. The macro is called "head", and you will notice how the date is automatically inserted. The person who designed this macro knows that Word-Perfect knows the date, set at the DOS level (see chapter 2), and just puts it in.

1. Ctrl→F10
2. heading <ret>
3. Shift→F6
4. Sara Jenkins <ret>
5. Shift→F6
6. 1235 Indiana Lane <ret>
7. Shift→F6

8. Lawrence, MA <ret>

9. Shift→F5,1 <ret>

10. press return

11. press return

12. Ctrl→F10

Step by step, this macro does the following.

- Step 1 turns on the macro feature
- Step 2 defines it as "heading"
- Step 3 centers the next line to be typed
- Step 4 enters the name
- Step 5 centers the next line to be typed
- Step 6 enters the street address
- Step 7 centers the next line to be typed
- Step 8 enters the city and state
- Step 9 enters the date (set by DOS)
- Step 10 enters a space
- Step 11 enters another space
- Step 12 ends the macro

Notice that step 9 enters whatever date was set when the computer system was booted up and the DOS system asked for a date. This means that the date set earlier will be the date printed here.

You can be as imaginative in using macros as you want. They are great time-savers and also a great deal of fun to use.

LESSON 18 EXERCISES

1. Think of five ways that you might be able to use macros in your everyday activities.

2. Design a macro named "greeting" in the exact same format as shown below and have it include the following information:
    your street address
    your city, state, and zip code
    today's date

    Dear   :

3   When these macros are invoked, what will be the outcome?
    Macro 1
    Ctrl→F10
    zipdel <ret>
    Alt→F4
    Home
    Home
    Down cursor arrow
    del
    Ctrl→F10

    Macro 2
    Ctrl→F10
    zipcheck <ret>
    Ctrl→F2,6
    Ctrl→F10

    Macro 3
    Ctrl→F10
    subcheck <ret>
    Alt→F2
    N
    Michael
    Alt→F2
    Paul
    Alt→F2
    Ctrl→F10

4. Design a macro that will automatically begin a document with marginal settings of 10 and 30 and double spacing.

5. Design a macro that will automatically bold face all the text in the document.

LESSON 19
Using WordPerfect Math

After this lesson you'll know:

- How to define a column as text or numeric.
- How to use operators such as " + " for addition, and " − " for subtraction.
- How to create a budget and compare it to actual expenses.

Important Terms

calculations   column definition   math

Important Keys

Alt→F7

As you have seen over the last 18 lessons, word processors can be used for many different things from writing memos to organizing lists to completing final reports. Some word processing programs, such as WordPerfect, can also do other things. In particular, WordPerfect **math** lets you perform several different kinds of mathematical calculations. For example, you might want to prepare, as part of a report, a budget which would involve addition and subtraction.

In general, you use WordPerfect math by first setting tabs that represent how columns will appear, defining the columns (or telling WordPerfect whether numbers or text will appear in them), turning the math function on, entering the numbers, and then calculating what you want.

Setting the Tabs

The first step in using WordPerfect math is to set tabs that allow you sufficient room to enter your numbers as columns. Figure 19–1 is the outline for a budget that will be used throughout this lesson to illustrate the use of WordPerfect math.

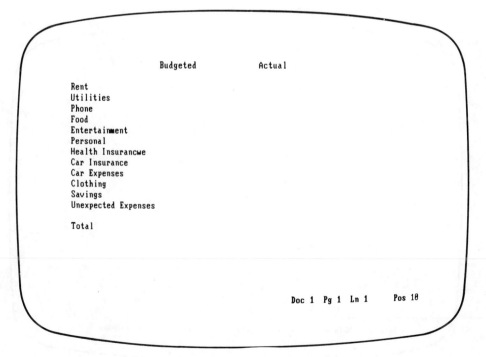

Figure 19–1　　A Budget

To set tabs, do the following.

1. Clear your WordPerfect screen.
2. Delete all previous tabs, as discussed in lesson 13.
3. Reset the tabs at 30 and 50, as shown in lesson 13.

After the tabs have been set, you can see how the cursor stops at columns 30 and 50 by pressing the tab key. These tab stops define the columns that will make up your budget.

WordPerfect Hint

Whenever you use WordPerfect math, you must be careful to allow enough room in each of the columns for all the numbers to be entered. For example, if you have a number with many digits (such as 123,456,789) you need tab stops at least 15 or 20 spaces apart. Otherwise,numbers will overlap and your computations will be incorrect.

Before you begin with the actual process of using WordPerfect math, the next step should be the creation of labels for the col-

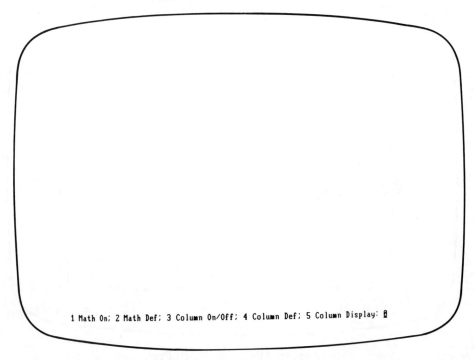

1 Math On; 2 Math Def; 3 Column On/Off; 4 Column Def; 5 Column Display: 0

Figure 19–2   WordPerfect Math Menu

umns. You don't need WordPerfect math to do this. Just use your WordPerfect skills to type in headings *Budgeted* and *Actual* as shown in figure 19–1.

Defining the Columns

Once you have set the tabs, the next step is to define the column using the **Alt→F7** key combination. When these keys are pressed, your WordPerfect screen should show the WordPerfect math menu as illustrated in figure 19–2. Since the next step in the process of using WordPerfect math is **column definition** you should choose option 2, Math Def.

When you select this option, WordPerfect will provide you with a screen, as shown in figure 19–3, which allows you to choose the *type* of column you want to use. In this case, it will be either a *text* column or a *numeric* column. In the budget example here, there are two columns. You can see how WordPerfect math can have up to 24 columns (A through X).

The second line in figure 19–3, Type, shows you what kind of column (text or numeric) WordPerfect has already defined. As you can see, the default is to set all columns as numeric (as indicated

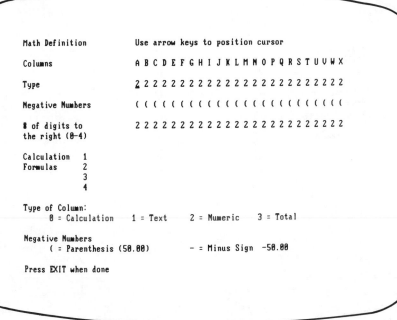

Figure 19–3   Math Definition Screen

by the number *2*). If you wanted a column to be text, then you would move the cursor arrow to that column and enter a 1.

WordPerfect math will not perform any operations on a column that is marked as a text column. When you are finished defining your columns, press the F7 key to exit back to the WordPerfect math menu.

Turning WordPerfect Math On

You should still have the WordPerfect math menu as shown in figure 19–2 at the bottom of your screen. Now select the option (1) that turns on WordPerfect math and you are ready to enter numbers that you will later use in **calculations**. When you turn on WordPerfect math, you will see the [Math On] code in the lower left-hand corner of your screen.

Entering Numbers and Operators

It's time to enter the information into your budget. Use the tab key to go to the column where you want to enter numerical data and

```
                    Budgeted        Actual

       Rent           250            250
       Utilities      100            110
       Phone           25             25
       Food           200            218
       Entertainment   50             42
       Personal        30             27
       Health Insurance 28            28
       Car Insurance   12             12
       Car Expenses    25             29
       Clothing        35             45
       Savings         50             50
       Unexpected Expenses 25         12

       Total           +              +




       Math                        Doc 2  Pg 1  Ln 16    Pos 19
```

Figure 19–4   A Budget, continued

enter the value. Don't forget to type in the general category as well, in the leftmost column of the budget. When you are finished entering data for any one row (such as *Rent* or *Food*), press the return key to go to the next category.

You'll notice that as you enter numbers, WordPerfect automatically aligns them in the column they are to be placed. This is very valuable for you, since it helps keep things in line and avoids any errors you might make in lining things up.

Just entering numbers would be fine, but WordPerfect does not know what you want to do with them unless you tell it. Since you want to add column entries together, your final entry in the *Budgeted* and *Actual* columns should be a plus (+) sign. Later on, when WordPerfect sees this sign, it will know to add the numbers in the column. Enter the numbers and the + operator as you see in figure 19–4. You can see that there are 12 different budget categories with a final Total at the bottom of each column.

Calculating Values

The last step in calculating your budget (and how well you did this month) is adding the columns. Your screen should look like the one

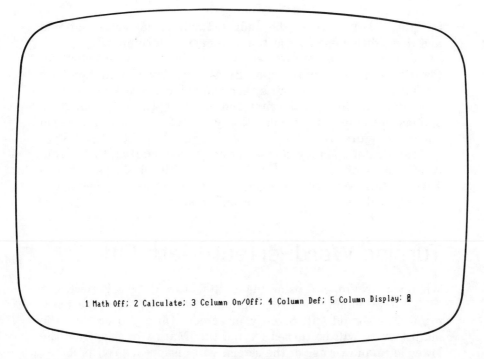

1 Math Off; 2 Calculate; 3 Column On/Off; 4 Column Def; 5 Column Display: 0

Figure 19–5   Math Menu for Columns

```
                   Budgeted           Actual


      Rent          250                250
      Utilities     100                110
      Phone          25                 25
      Food          200                218
      Entertainment  50                 42
      Personal       30                 27
      Health Insurance 28               28
      Car Insurance  12                 12
      Car Expenses   25                 29
      Clothing       35                 45
      Savings        50                 50
      Unexpected Expenses 25            12

      Total         830.00             848.00




      Math                          Doc 1  Pg 1  Ln 17     Pos 30
```

Figure 19–6   A Budget, $18 over!

in figure 19–4, with all the budgeted and actual values entered and the addition operator at the bottom of each column.

To calculate column totals, you need to go to a second Word-Perfect math menu by pressing the Alt→F7 key combination once again. At the bottom of your screen, you will see a new math menu (see figure 19–5) with the first and second options replacing the options on the first math menu that you used earlier in this lesson (shown in figure 19–2).

To calculate, simply choose option 2 (calculate) on that menu. After a moment, you will see the finished table, as shown in figure 19–6. If this were your budget, you would have overspent your monthly budget by a relatively small amount.

Turning WordPerfect Math Off

When you are finished using the math feature of WordPerfect, you cancel it by simply selecting option 1 *Math Off* from the math menu that should still be on your screen. Once you do this, the math feature will be turned off and the [Math On] code from the lower left-hand corner of the screen will disappear. You probably would now want to save your work as a file.

LESSON 19 EXERCISES

1. Use WordPerfect math to create a matrix of numbers that has four rows and four columns as shown below and enter 16 one digit numbers.

		Column			
		1	2	3	4
	1	2	6	7	8
	2	4	5	4	3
Row	3	7	6	8	3
	4	5	4	3	4

TOTALS

2. Using the matrix you created above, use WordPerfect's global features to change all the 4s to 3s, and then recalculate the totals.

3. Name five uses of the WordPerfect math feature, including at least one in which you need to incorporate it into an already existing text file.

a)

b)

c)

d)

e)

PART III

WordPerfect and Everyday Needs

Word processors can be used for many different things. Throughout parts I and II of *Mastering WordPerfect*, you have learned about some of WordPerfect's most often used features. But besides these applications, there are others that are equally useful. These other applications are the focus of part III of *Mastering WordPerfect*.

Ever want to send the same letter to 20 people without writing and addressing each one separately, write a personal or business letter that communicates what you want it to say, deliver an outstanding resume? While you can do any of these with most word processing programs, WordPerfect, and some hints about writing, will help you see outstanding results!

Writing Personalized Letters

After this chapter you'll know

- How to create a primary file.
- How to create a secondary file.
- How to use the merge commands menu.
- How to merge files together to produce personalized letters.

Important Terms

field	merge commands	secondary file
merge	primary file	

Anyone who writes letters will, at one time or another, end up having to send the *same* letter to many different people. Wouldn't it be nice if you could *personalize* each of these letters, so that all the people receive a letter addressed just to them?

WordPerfect (and you) can do this with ease using the **merge** feature, which is described below.

First, you create what WordPerfect calls a **secondary file**. This file will contain **fields** such as the names, addresses, and any other information that you want to use in the personalized letters you are sending. Next, create what WordPerfect calls a **primary file**. This file contains the letter that will be combined with the personal information from the secondary file.

Once these are created and saved, WordPerfect can then merge the two files to produce personalized letters. Here is an example of how a secondary and primary file can be created for someone who would like to order a camping catalog from three separate stores.

Creating a Secondary File

To create a secondary file of three catalog companies, follow these steps.

1. Type in the name of the first company and press the F9 key. The ˆR symbol lets WordPerfect know that this ends a field.

2. Type in the street address of the first company and press the F9 key.

3. Type in the city, state, and zip code of the first company and press the F9 key. When you have entered these three fields, ending each one by pressing the F9 key, your screen should look like the one in figure 20–1.

4. After you have entered the last field and advanced to the next line (using the <F9> key), press the Shift→F9 key combination (which places a ˆE at the end of the record). The first record is now complete.

5. Now repeat this process with the two other companies to produce the file shown in figure 20–2.

6. Save this file under the name "add.sf". The *sf* extension stands for secondary file.

Creating a Primary File

The next file to create is the actual letter requesting a catalog. It will be merged with the addresses stored in the secondary file.

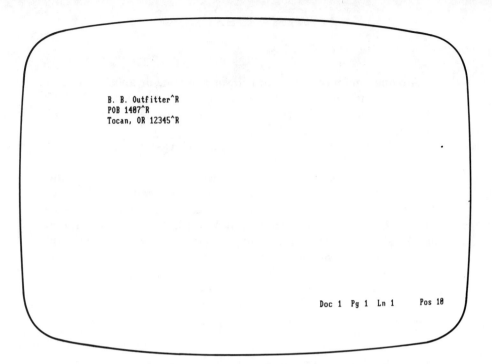

```
        B. B. Outfitter^R
        POB 1407^R
        Tocan, OR 12345^R
```

```
                                            Doc 1  Pg 1  Ln 1     Pos 18
```

Figure 20–1   A Secondary File of Addresses

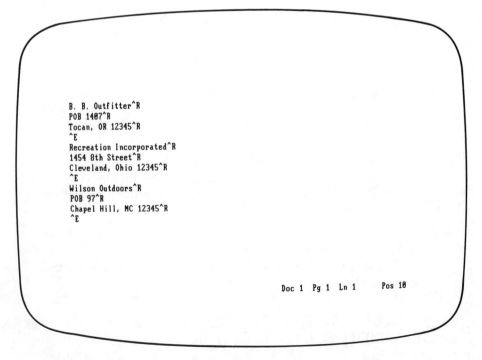

```
        B. B. Outfitter^R
        POB 1407^R
        Tocan, OR 12345^R
        ^E
        Recreation Incorporated^R
        1454 8th Street^R
        Cleveland, Ohio 12345^R
        ^E
        Wilson Outdoors^R
        POB 97^R
        Chapel Hill, NC 12345^R
        ^E
```

```
                                            Doc 1  Pg 1  Ln 1     Pos 18
```

Figure 20–2   The Completed Secondary File

To create a primary file, follow these steps.

1. Press the Alt→F9 key combination to produce the **merge codes menu** that appears in figure 20–3. These are all the symbols you need to insert into a file to have the WordPerfect merge function work properly.

2. Press the F,1,<ret> sequence of keys, which will produce the F1 code as the first line in your letter. When it comes time to merge the two files, WordPerfect will know that the first field you defined in the secondary file (using the R) code will be placed here. Press the return key once again to separate the sets of names and addresses.

3. To place the code for the second field, press the Alt→F9 key combination, and then the F,2,<ret>,<ret> sequence of keys to produce the F2 code for the second field.

4. To place the code for the third and last field, press Alt→F9 and then the F,3,<ret>,<ret> sequence of keys to produce the F3 code for the third field. Your final screen should look like the one in figure 20–4.

    Notice that you have as many fields defined in the primary

^C; ^D; ^F; ^G; ^N; ^O; ^P; ^Q; ^S; ^T; ^U; ^V: _

Figure 20–3   The Merge Codes Menu

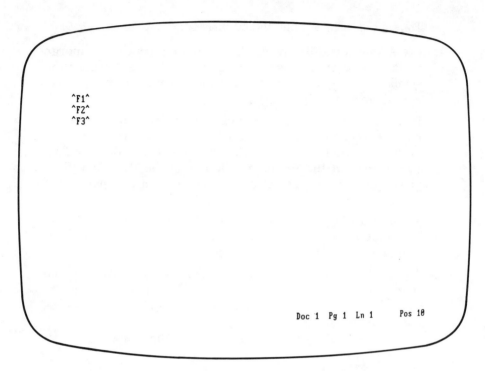

```
^F1^
^F2^
^F3^




                                            Doc 1  Pg 1  Ln 1      Pos 10
```

Figure 20–4   Merge Codes in the Primary File

file as you entered in the secondary file. One of the rules of the WordPerfect merge feature is that the number of fields defined in any one record in the secondary file and the number of merge codes in the primary file *must* be the same.

5. Now you can write the body of the primary file, which is a letter requesting a catalog. The complete primary file appears in figure 20–5. After it is completed, save it under the name "letter.pf". The extension *pf* stands for primary file.

You should now have two files, ready to be merged to produce three separate, individually addressed letters.

Merging a Primary and Secondary File

Before you begin merging the two files, be sure your WordPerfect screen is cleared.

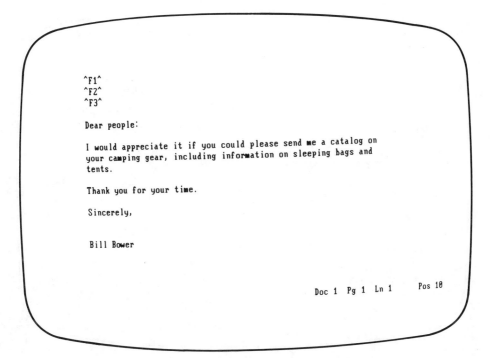

```
^F1^
^F2^
^F3^

Dear people:

I would appreciate it if you could please send me a catalog on
your camping gear, including information on sleeping bags and
tents.

Thank you for your time.

Sincerely,


Bill Bower



                                          Doc 1  Pg 1  Ln 1      Pos 10
```

Figure 20-5   The Completed Primary File

To merge the two files, follow these steps.

1. Press the Ctrl→F9,1 combination of keys to select the Word-
    Perfect merge function, and you will see the following message,
    asking you for the name of the primary file you want to merge.

    Primary file:

    Enter the name "letter.pf" and press the return key.

2. WordPerfect will now ask you to supply the name of the sec-
    ondary file, asking you

    Secondary file:

    Enter the name "add.sf" and press the return key. WordPerfect
    will automatically create a file of the merged letters and dis-
    play them on the screen.

3. Save this merged file (which is a combination of the primary
    file and secondary file) under the name "catalog.ltr". This way
    you know it is the letter requesting catalogs.

4. The final file should look like the one shown in figure 20–6,
    with a hard page break (two dotted lines) separating each of
    the letters.

```
B. B. Outfitter
POB 1407
Tocan, OR 12345

Dear people:

I would appreciate it if you could please send me a catalog on
your camping gear, including information on sleeping bags and
tents.

Thank you for your time.

Sincerely,


Bill Bower
===========================================================================
Recreation Incorporated
1454 8th Street
Cleveland, Ohio 12345
                                    Doc 1  Pg 1  Ln 1      Pos 10
```

Figure 20–6   The Personalized Letters

5. To print out the letter, simply print the files (Shift→F7,1) and
    you'll have your three letters, personalized and printed!

Other Things To Merge

You can personalize letters and specialize documents in any way
you want, depending on how you design the primary and secondary
files. Like other WordPerfect features, what you can do is only limited by your imagination and ingenuity. For example, if you
wanted to write to each of these three catalog companies, often, but
request specific information on a *different* item from each one, you
would need to add an extra field to each of the records in the secondary file. You would also need a place for that field to appear in
the primary file.

Figure 20–7 shows you this new secondary file with the new
added fields highlighted.

Figure 20–8 shows you the new primary file with the fourth
merge code imbedded in the actual text of the letter.

Figure 20–9 shows you an example of what the first merged
letter looks like after the primary and secondary files are joined.

```
B. B. Outfitter^R
POB 1407^R
Tocan, OR 12345^R
dome tents^R
^E
Recreation Incorporated^R
1454 8th Street^R
Cleveland, Ohio 12345^R
pop-up tents^R
^E
Wilson Outdoors^R
POB 97^R
Chapel Hill, NC 12345^R
backpacking tents^R
^E

                                          Doc 1  Pg 1  Ln 1      Pos 10
```

Figure 20–7 The New Secondary File with Four Fields

```
^F1^
^F2^
^F3^

Dear people:

I would appreciate it if you could please send me information on
your ^F4^ since I am considering purchasing one for an upcoming
trip.

Thank you for your time.

Sincerely,


Bill Bower


                                          Doc 1  Pg 1  Ln 1      Pos 10
```

Figure 20–8 The Completed Primary File

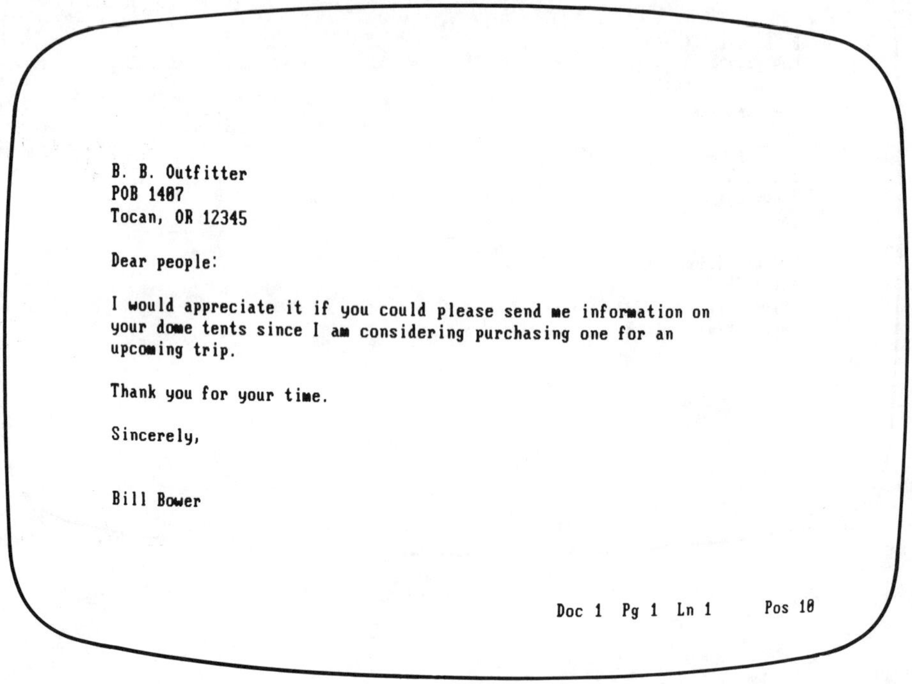

```
B. B. Outfitter
POB 1407
Tocan, OR 12345

Dear people:

I would appreciate it if you could please send me information on
your dome tents since I am considering purchasing one for an
upcoming trip.

Thank you for your time.

Sincerely,


Bill Bower




                                        Doc 1  Pg 1  Ln 1      Pos 10
```

Figure 20–9   The First Merged Letter

LESSON 20 EXERCISES

1. Send the following memo to the people listed below. Be sure to personalize the letter using the WordPerfect merge feature by including the information about each person's raise.

   [NAME]
   Department of Education
   University of Missouri
   Columbia, MO

   Dear [NAME]:

   Once again, it is time for me to decide merit salary increases. I am pleased to report that your raise for the following year is [PERCENT].

   Best wishes,

   John Poyo

   Send this memo to:

Reva James	15%
Larry Hairston	1%
Doug Windom	12%
Marvin LeDou	10%

2. What would happen if you had more fields specified in your secondary file than you provided room for in your primary file? What would be one way to check this before you merge the fields?

3. You have just merged a secondary and a primary file to produce 10 personalized letters. You discovered, however, that the city used in the address is spelled incorrectly. How can you correct this problem without going back and changing each of the entries in the secondary file?

Writing with a Word Processor

After this lesson you'll know

- What makes a good writer.
- What the POWER system of writing with a word processor is.
- How using WordPerfect can make you a better writer.

Well, here you are. An accomplished WordPerfect user who is ready to begin using WordPerfect whenever possible. That's the attitude you really need to have, since practice makes perfect. The more you use WordPerfect, the better you will be at using it. There's also one other important benefit: you're on your way to becoming a better, and maybe even a good, writer.

What's a good writer? It's someone who does many other things besides spell properly and use the correct punctuation. Good writers have a beginning, a middle, and end to what they write, regardless of whether they're writing a simple letter or a 20-page term paper. The paragraphs they write have a singular important thought in mind, and the different paragraphs (and thoughts) are related to each other through some common theme. Good writers also organize their writing so it is clear and to the point, without rambling on about other things that are unrelated to the topic of the paper.

Can you produce good writing? Of course. Anyone can who is willing to *practice*. If you wanted to be a masterful violin player, you would practice. If you wanted to be a star basketball player, you would practice. It's the same with writing. While not everyone has the "gift" of being an excellent writer, anyone can certainly learn to communicate his or her thoughts clearly and become a better writer.

Practicing with POWER

Many systems have been developed to help people become better writers. One that many word processing users have found especially helpful was developed by Gwen Solomon in her book *Writing With a Word Processor*. She lists five steps to good writing with a word processor:

*P*re-writing

*O*rganize

*W*riting

*E*xchange

*R*evising

The first step to effective writing is to generate as many ideas as you can about the topic. This stage of *pre-writing* might include going to the library for information, interviewing experts about a certain area, or just spending time thinking about the project. This is the time for you to generate as many ideas as possible. When

you are at the pre-writing stage, don't be concerned about the quality of your ideas, that is, whether they are good or bad. As you
work through these points, and try to fit them into your overall
theme, the goods ones will stand out and the bad ones will fade
into the background.

After you have generated lots of ideas, both good and bad, the
next step is to *organize* these into some kind of an order that communicates what you want to express. An outline using Word-
Perfect (see lesson 17), is an excellent first step in this process.
While not everyone works with outlines, many writers find them
indispensible. You can then follow that outline as you write, making changes in the order of presentation of ideas, as the writing
develops. Don't be concerned if your outline needs to be reworked
as you go along. You may find that one point is very important,
but just doesn't belong in the place where it is.

The third step of Solomon's system, *writing* is where you actually put the words down "on paper" (or on screen!). Now is the
time when the creative pre-writing phase and the organization
should all come together to produce the *first draft* of a document.
For most beginning writers, it's generally true that the more time
you invest in generating and, especially, organizing thoughts and
ideas, the better the first draft will be.

What do you do when that first draft is done? Get some feedback from friends, colleagues, teachers and anyone else who will
exchange drafts and read your writing and then talk with you
about it. In turn, you will be expected to read other people's drafts
and give them feedback. This is a valuable service to perform, and
one from which you can learn a handsome amount as well. Seeing
other people's mistakes can help you avoid making the same ones.

OK, your first draft is finished and you just got it back from
the classmate you know will give you the feedback you need
("Some of these points don't seem to go together.") versus the feedback you want ("I loved it!"). Now what?

It's time to address those points in the *revision* and the production of the *second, third,* and however many drafts it takes to get
your paper to a place that you feel it is the best that you can do.
You don't need to react to every single comment that anyone
makes on your work, since some might just be other people's opin-
ions (e.g., "I don't like the name of the main character." or "The
civil war is boring."). You have to judge for yourself what comments are important.

Some Word Processing and Writing Tips

Writers have produced thousands of words using word processors and along the way have picked up some very helpful ideas. Here are just some of these pointers.

One thing you could do right off to be a better word processor user and writer, is to be a better typist. After all, the keyboard on your computer is just like a typewriter keyboard. The more accurate and quicker you are on this keyboard, the more productive you will be, even if your writing has a way to go. If you are not a competent typist, enroll in a typing course. Typing is a lifelong skill that you will never regret developing.

Be sure that you have sufficient light where you are working so that both the screen and your reference materials are easy to read.

While on the subject of light, if you do a lot of word processing, you might find it helpful to buy some kind of a non-glare screen for your monitor. This helps reduce the amount of light reflected off the screen and cuts down eye fatigue and strain, letting you work and stay fresh longer.

And speaking of fatigue, don't work for very long sessions until you know your limits. Work for 30 or 40 minutes and then take a break. Even if WordPerfect is "bulletproof," and will not allow you to make a fatal mistake such as erasing a file, the likelihood of a mistake happening increases as you grow tired.

The WordPerfect search and replace function can be a wonderful time saver. For example, you are writing a paper about a new medical discovery and the chemical *desoxyribonucleic* acid is mentioned various times. Would you rather type that in every time, or simply use the abbreviation DNA and then search for it and replace it with the full name? There's no comparison in the number of keystrokes and the gain in accuracy from using search and replace. When this book was written, the word *WordPerfect* was typed as "wp." Then, with one global search and replace, it was changed throughout some 400 pages!

Use as many *macros* (lesson 18) as you can. For example, you can use a macro to do a heading on your letters as well as the salutation. You can also use one to incorporate a copyright statement on the cover page of a document, like this;

Copyright, 1987, [your name]

You might even find yourself using a macro to repeat an entire paragraph when that information needs to be used over and over again.

Always back up your work. When you are finished with one day's writing, copy the file (or files) onto another formatted disk. At the end of each work session, you should have two identical disks. One disk is the work disk that you work with everyday, and the other is a duplicate copy of that work disk that you have for safekeeping should something happen to the first disk or to a file on that disk.

Don't be overconfident. Everyone, and that means you as well, at one time or another accidentally erases something on a disk or even manages to erase the contents of an entire disk. Horrors! While there are computer program utilities that can help you re-cover what is lost, it is cheaper and certainly less aggravating to take your back up and go from there. Your DOS (disk operating system) manual contains information on backing up disks.

Writing the Perfect Letter and Resume

After this lesson you'll know

- Why a good cover letter and well prepared resume are so important in finding a job.
- How to use WordPerfect to create a letter and resume to give you a special advantage as you look for employment.

Dear Mr. Smith,

   I saw your ad in the paper yesterday and the job you
described looks terrific.

I'll be giving you a call this week about my application. How
many references do I need and what should I ask them to
send you. Thanks you for your time.

Thanks,

Pat Walkton

                    ****

                     John Elhi
                  1235 Tenth Street
                    Buffalo, NY

December 1, 1986

Mr. William Smith
Co-op City Workers
POB 8713
Tampa, FL

Dear Mr. Smith:

I read with great interest your advertisement in last Sunday's
Herald Examiner for a building superintendent. For the past
ten years, I have been a building supervisor in a large
Northeast city but plan to relocate to your area if I can find
suitable employment.

Please find enclosed my application for the position and a
summary of my experience. I will be calling you next week
when I am in the area to see if I can visit with you and we
can talk.

Thank you in advance for your time.

Sincerely,

John Elhi

   If you were looking for a new supervisor, which person would
you interview? Wouldn't it be John, since his letter is so well organized and to the point. He prepared it carefully (no typos or

spelling errors), has his name and address clearly stated at the top, and offers more information if needed.

First Impressions

A good letter contains many different elements, all of which contribute to effective communication. The message is, of course, important, but how it looks can often make the difference between just "a letter" and successful communication of your ideas. First, since people get their initial impression about a letter by the way that it looks and feels, use the right kind of paper.

The Paper

The quality of paper is reflected in its *rag* content, which is actually the percent of cotton fiber in the paper. The more cotton fiber, the better the quality. Paper also comes in different weights (15 pound, 20 pound, etc.). The heavier the paper, the better the quality as well. It's no surprise that people who know how to write an effective letter choose a paper with a high weight (20 pound or more) and with a high rag content (from 50 to 100%). These papers are more expensive, but are much more durable and give the impression you want to communicate something important.

Never use what is called *onion skin* paper, which is thin, almost transparent paper. It is light and flimsy, as well as difficult to read.

Finally, you can probably use either single sheets or fanfold paper in your printer. Single sheets are individual pieces of paper. Fanfold paper is sheets of paper attached to each other with those funny sprocket holes run up the sides. The holes guide the paper through a printer.

If you do choose fanfold paper, be sure that you choose the kind that cleanly separates from other sheets, as well as from the sprocket guide on the sides. Some of this paper's trade names are "Kleen Edge" and "Micro-Perf." When these sheets are separated, it's difficult to tell that they were not individually cut sheets of paper.

Size and Color

The generally accepted size for letters is 8-1/2 by 11 inches, which fits neatly into a #10 envelope. While different people have a preference for color, most letters should be written on white paper. You don't want the color of the paper to distract from what the letter has to say.

The Letterhead

While you could spend lots of money having a graphics artist design your own letterhead, working with WordPerfect and macros you can incorporate your own letterhead into all of your letters.

In lesson 18 you learned how to set up a macro to produce a heading on demand. All you need to do is invoke the macro and you have your own heading. In figure 22–1 you can see some sample headings that you might find attractive. They are all easy to enter and to use as a macro.

You can even split the letterhead, by having the name at the top and the actual address at the bottom, with the body of the letter placed in between. An example of this style is shown in figure 22–2.

Presentation

Letters can be presented in a *blocked* or *unblocked* style, as shown by the comparison in figure 22–3. The blocked style has everything aligned on the left-hand margin, including addresses, dates, and

```
                        ********
                       David Kass
                    1428 14th Street
                    Washington, DC


   Consultant        Inventor       Trouble-Shooter
                        ********




                        ********
                    Jack Jordan, Esq.

   1515 Third Avenue                  2 Ridge Court
       NY, NY                          Paston, CT
   (212) 749–0946                    (203) 445–0990
                        ********
```

Figure 22–1   Sample Letterheads

```
                        ********
                   Michael P. Smith
                    Attorney at Law

                    [letter here]


 457 Westridge Road     Columbus, Ohio      (614) 657–8957
                        ********
```

Figure 22–2   A Split Letterhead

text. The unblocked style has dates set off (often centered as the example shows) with paragraphs indented.

Hellos and Goodbyes

The way you open and close a letter may be as important as the content. You should use the type of closing that fits the circumstances of the letter. If you need a *formal* greeting for a job application or a letter of interest in a service, the salutation should be something like this:

Dear Ms. Willson:

Notice the use of the "Ms." title. This assumes that you don't know the marital status of the woman. The use of the colon is a formal gesture.

An *informal* greeting includes first names and the use of a comma:

Dear Willy,

conveying a much more relaxed atmosphere.

<u>The Blocked Style</u>

January 5, 1985

Ms. Leni Willis
18 Stering Avenue
Jersey City, NJ

Dear Ms. Willis:

I was very pleased to learn that you were considering our company
in your employment plans. I am sure that if you chose to work
for us, you will find it exciting and rewarding.

Along with this letter, I am enclosing some forms that you need
to complete as well as some information about living in the
metropolitan New York area. If you have any question, please
contact me at your convenience.

Sincerely,

N. Joseph Sacks
Personnel
                                Doc 1 Pg 1 Ln 29   Pos 18

<u>The Unblocked Style</u>

                  January 5, 1985

Ms. Leni Willis
18 Stering Avenue
Jersey City, NJ

Dear Ms. Willis:

      I was very pleased to learn that you were considering our
company in your employment plans. I am sure that if you chose to
work for us, you will find it exciting and rewarding.

      Along with this letter, I am enclosing some forms that you
need to complete as well as some information about living in the
metropolitan New York area. If you have any question, please
contact me at your convenience.

Sincerely,
N. Joseph Sacks
Personnel
                                Doc 1 Pg 2 Ln 24   Pos 18

Figure 22–3   Blocked and Unblocked Letter Styles

Just as salutations can be formal or informal, so can closings. Some examples of highly formal closings are:

Yours very truly,
Very truly yours,
Respectfully yours,

Some examples of personal closings are:

Sincerely,
Cordially,
Sincerely yours,

Some very informal closings are:

Best wishes,
Your friend,
See you soon!

The important thing is that the salutation and closing fit the tone of the letter.

Spacing and Margins

Almost all letters, whether for business or not, are single spaced with a blank line between each paragraph. This makes for a pleasing appearance without any wasting of space.

Be sure, however, that before you print out a letter, that a *page break* does not come at an inconvenient place. For example, what if your letter was just over one page long and the word processor automatically advanced to the next page just before it typed the salutation? This is shown in figure 22–4.

One way (and perhaps the easiest) to correct this problem is to make the margins shorter (and then you'll have more lines on page one and some on page two as well). Another way is to force a *page break* (Ctrl→Return) after the last paragraph on page one, pushing the last paragraph onto page two. In figure 22–5, you can see how a page break was placed right before the last full paragraph.

Writing the Perfect Resume

A resume is a summary of your job qualifications. Many people feel that the purpose of a resume is to get an employer to invite you for an interview or to talk with you about the position for which you are applying.

One of the primary reasons why you will find WordPerfect so helpful in preparing a resume is that it allows you to *tailor* your resume to each of the employers you might be contacting. For ex-

```
                    Dr. Mike Ganeson
                        POB 1327
                    Williamstown, ME


February 24, 1986

Mr. Don Simpson, Editor
Smith Magazine
900 Thurber Avenue
Washington, DC 20560

Dear Mr. Simpson:

I am currently working on a manuscript on supercomputers as
described in the attached query and would like to know if Career
Magazine would consider reviewing it for possible publication.
As an associate of the Career Foundation, I have received the
magazine for years and feel that the general and timely content
of the mss. would appeal to your readers.

I have been writing about computers for the last five years with
articles in Computing Fun, Micro, and lead articles in several
issues of PROGRAM magazine, which has a circulation of over
                                   Doc 1  Pg 1  Ln 6      Pos 10
```

```
200,000.  A major strength of my writing is that I take technical
concepts and translate them into language that lay audiences
understand and appreciate.  For your information, I am including
a copy of my vita as well as some representative clips of
articles that I have published.

On another matter, I am a friend and colleague of Dr. Robert
Stanton, soon to be new director of your research division. I
know that in the past you have had profile articles of new
directors and was wondering if you would like to consider one in
this case.  Being in Williamstown, I would have access to Bob for
interviews as well as information about his scholarship and his
museum work here. I have already discussed the possibility with
him and he was very interested.
================================================================

Sincerely,


                                   Doc 1  Pg 2  Ln 8      Pos 10
```

Figure 22–4   Poorly Spaced Page Break

```
                Dr. Mike Ganeson
                   POB 1327
                Williamstown, ME


    February 24, 1986

    Mr. Don Simpson, Editor
    Smith Magazine
    900 Thurber Avenue
    Washington, DC 20560

    Dear Mr. Simpson:

    I am currently working on a manuscript on
    supercomputers as described in the attached
    query and would like to know if Career
    Magazine would consider reviewing it for
    possible publication.  As an associate of the
    Career Foundation, I have received the
    magazine for years and feel that the general
    and timely content of the mss. would appeal to
    your readers.
    I have been writing about computers for the
    last five years with articles in Computing
    Fun, Micro, and lead articles in several
    issues of PROGRAM magazine, which has a

                                    Doc 1  Pg 3  Ln 13     POS 10
```

```
    circulation of over 200,000.  A major strength
    of my writing is that I take technical
    concepts and translate them into language that
    lay audiences understand and appreciate.  For
    your information, I am including a copy of my
    vita as well as some representative clips of
    articles that I have published.
    =========================================================================
    On another matter, I am a friend and colleague
    of Dr. Robert Stanton, soon to be new director
    of your research division. I know that in the
    past you have had profile articles of new
    directors and was wondering if you would like
    to consider one in this case.  Being in
    Williamstown, I would have access to Bob for
    interviews as well as information about his
    scholarship and his museum work here. I have
    already discussed the possibility with him and
    he was very interested.


    Sincerely,



    Mike Ganeson
                                    Doc 1  Pg 4  Ln 21     POS 23
```

Figure 22–5   Adjusting the Page Break

ample, you might want to emphasize a certain type of qualification for one employer (your extensive experience working in stores), while, for another, you might want to describe how much time you have spent supervising others. With a word processor, you can rearrange and emphasize different things with ease.

There are many different forms of a resume. For example, the basic form fits many people's needs. But there are also the *chronological* resume (listing things in order of when they happened), the *creative* resume (in which the writer uses his or her own specialized way of presenting material), and the *functional* resume (where activities are listed by what was involved), among many others.

What's In the Basic Resume?

A simple resume has four basic parts: a *heading,* a summary of your *education,* a summary of any *experiences* that are relevant to the job, and *references.* More complex resumes also include personal information (age, health, etc.), objective (what kind of a position you want), salary needs, preference for location, when you will be available, and outside interests.

What follows is a discussion of each of the four simple types, responding to the following classified ad that appeared in a local newspaper.

> ASSISTANT RESEARCHER. Small independent research firm located outside a large city on the West Coast needs a beginning research assistant to do work in the development of educational programs in the area of elementary school science. Must have college degree and some general experience in science and computers. Excellent salary and benefits with a chance to grow with the company. Send letter of interest and resume to Box 999 care of this paper.

Heading

A heading is an introduction of sorts, much like the letterhead on a letter. It should contain your name, address, phone number, and the name of the position for which you are applying. You can see in the following example, how WordPerfect's centering feature was used for these first five lines of text:

Richard Eisen
2627 ValVerde Road
Oakland, CA
(215) 334-7689

for the position of *Assistant Researcher*

This gives the potential employer a quick summary of who you are, and most importantly, how to reach you. Be sure that you proofread whatever you type to be sure that addresses, and especially phone numbers, are correct.

Education

Your potential employer will want to know about your educational background, and how that might relate to the position. The classified ad asks for someone who has a college degree, without specifying the applicant's major area of study.

If you did study a science, it would be to your advantage to emphasize this, by perhaps listing the courses that you took that are related to science or to computers. For example, the second part of your resume could look like this:

B.A. Biology, Arizona State University, 1985

Courses in: Basic computer science
             Anatomy
             Chemistry
             Physics

If you didn't get a degree in an area that focuses on the sciences, don't despair. List any courses that might relate to what the job description sounds like it may require. For example, let's say that you were a history major, but also took a class in child development. This might be to your advantage, since the advertisement mentions elementary education. In this case, your resume could look like this:

B.A. History, University of Maryland, 1981.

Courses in: Child Development
             History of Children
             Editing Texts

While these courses might not be as directly related to the job description as the ones mentioned earlier, a potential employer might look upon them favorably if he or she feels that your degree in history and courses taken in child development would make you a better overall candidate.

What if you have absolutely no relevant or even indirectly related educational qualifications? Do the best you can and *de-emphasize* this section by placing it after the summary of your experiences, which comes next.

Experiences

Just as with education, you should frame your experiences in such a way as to make you look like a very attractive candidate for the position.

The advertisement for the research assistant is looking for someone who has some general experience in science and computers. This can mean anything from owning your own personal computer to helping teach word processing to someone else! You want to emphasize how your experiences might relate to the kind of job described in the advertisement.

For example, a summary of experiences might look like this:

> Experience
>
> Worked as sales person at Personal Computer Center
> every holiday season for the past four years. I
> not only sold computers and printers and
> accessories, but also demonstrated word processing
> programs for interested customers.
>
> Assisted in the testing of a new program that
> checks the spelling of foreign words.
>
> Subscribe to Science & You, a monthly magazine for
> the amateur scientist.

Try to make everything you have done work for you.

References

References may be the most important part of any resume, since they can make or break your opportunity to get your foot in the door for an interview. There are several important things to remember about choosing a reference to be listed.

List those people you think will give you a very positive reference. Write a letter to your references telling them of your intentions to apply for a particular job and ask them if you can use their name as a reference. You might want to include a copy of the job description, as well as a copy of the resume you intend to send to the employer.

Second, ask them directly if they feel that they can give you a good reference. Even though you think these people might be able to speak of you in glowing terms, you never know what they are going to say. Most letters of reference are confidential, so you will probably not be able to see what a reference has written about you. It may be awkward, but you have to be sure that he or she will speak of you in positive terms.

Richard Eisen
2627 ValVerde Road
Oakland, CA
(215) 334–7689

Education

B.A. Biology, Arizona State University, 1985

Courses in: Basic computer science
Anatomy
Chemistry
Physics

Experience

Worked as sales person at Personal Computer
Center every holiday season for the past four years.
I not only sold computers, printers and accesories,
but also demonstrated word processing programs for
interested customers.

Assisted in the testing of a new program that
checks the spelling of foreign words.

Subscribe to Science & You, a monthly magazine
for the amateur scientist.

References

Fret, B. Owner and operator, Personal Computer
Center, 417 8th Street, Oakland, California, 90031,
(215) 657–6645.

Wilson, T. Faculty member in the Department of
Biology, Arizona State University, Tempe, Arizona,
56656, (231) 431–0990.

Anderson, B. Faculty member in the Department of
Biology, Arizona State University, Tempe, Arizona,
56656, (231) 431–7876.

Figure 22–6   Richard's Resume

Third, ask the reference to address your qualifications in light of the job requirements. This way, he or she can emphasize what you can do well that is directly relevant to what the employer might want.

Finally, don't ever ask someone to write you a reference who does not know your work. You will end up with a neutral recommendation at best, leaving the employer thinking you are neither here nor there.

You can see in figure 22–6 the completed resume with the references at the end. Notice how the references are listed completely, including names and addresses.

Finishing the Resume

Just as with any other typed materials, the nicer the resume looks, the more effective it will be. When you are ready to produce the final copy of your resume, keep the following things in mind.

First, check the *spelling*. There is probably nothing that will detract from an otherwise outstanding resume more than spelling errors.

Second, the resume should be *no more than 2 pages long*. The purpose of a resume is to provide a summary of your education and experience, not a detailed biography of everything you have done.

Third, have your resume printed on a printer that can give you *letter quality* type. The results will look like your resume was typed using the best quality typewriter. Also, use a good white paper with a high rag content for printing.

Finally, when you mail your resume to a potential employer, do not fold it. Instead use a large envelope; this looks more professional.

PART IV

WordPerfect
Extras

Glossary

append block attaching a block of text to the end of an existing file

Arabic numerals 1, 2, 3, etc

back space key key that moves the cursor back one space

backup disk an exact duplicate of an existing file or document

backward search searching through a file from the end of the document to the beginning of the document for a specific set of characters

block a defined area of a document that can be printed, deleted, saved, or acted upon using almost any WordPerfect command

bold emphasized letters

calculations WordPerfect math option that allows you to total columns, as in keeping a budget

centering when text is centered between margins

change directory going from one directory and/or disk to another, usually done using the list files feature

character position indicator indicates in which column the cursor is located

clearing the screen creating a blank WordPerfect screen, usually for beginning or retrieving a new document

clone an exact copy

column definition feature of WordPerfect math that lets you set up columns of any width for math work

compatible a computer that can operate software designed for another computer

continuous double underlining two continuous unbroken lines underneath text (not all printers can do this)

continuous single underlining one continuous unbroken line beneath text

copy block copying blocked text into another part of a document

create to begin a new file

cursor the blinking symbol on the monitor screen indicating your position on the monitor screen

cursor keys the set of keys on the numeric key pad that controls the action of the cursor

cut block deleting a block of text

default value a preset value that WordPerfect always reverts to if not given any other directions

delete to erase or remove from the monitor screen or file, using the delete key

destination the location where you intend to store something

dictionary the WordPerfect file that stores the correct spelling of words

direction arrows control keys that move the cursor from line to line and character to character

disk drive the device that spins the disk so information can be read by the computer

disk operating system the system that provides operating instructions for the computer

document cursor movement movement of the cursor from document to document using the cursor keys

document indicator the number in the lower left-hand corner of the screen indicating the number of the document currently active

DOS an abbreviation for Disk Operating System

edit to change text, such as from "dukc" to "duck"

elite a typeface with 12 characters per inch

esc a keyboard command that sets the number of times an operation, such as a macro, will be performed

exiting leaving WordPerfect when you no longer want to continue working with the word processor

extension the letters following the period after the file name

field sections from different documents that can be merged, such as addresses and the text of a letter

file a unique set of information stored on a disk

file name the name assigned to a file, usually containing an extension, such as "bill.ltr"

floppy disk a type of magnetic media that stores information so it can be read using a disk drive

font a style of letter

format the physical appearance of a document including spacing, margins, tabs, number of lines per page, and more

forward search searching through a file from the beginning of a document to the end of a document for a set of characters

front matter the material in a book, such as the table of contents, preface, etc., that appears before the actual text

full text option the print menu option to print the entire document

function keys ten keys, each of which performs a particular function

global search and replace searching through an entire document for a certain occurrence and automatically changing it to something else

hard copy a permanent copy of a document on paper

hard disk a rigid type of computer storage media

headers and footers printed lines appearing on the tops and bottoms of document pages

headings names of the different levels in an outline

Help The F1 key that provides a copy of the function keys and what they do

highlight when text appears in reverse video

input providing the computer with information to act on

insert mode when new text is inserted between existing characters

internal dictionary the list of words that WordPerfect uses to check spelling/typing accuracy

italics slanted letters

K a unit of storage for computers of about 1,000 characters

label the name of a file or disk

left margin the position along which the left-hand side of the text will be aligned

levels different steps of an outline, from most important to less important

line cursor movement movement of the cursor from line to line using the cursor keys

line format the way in which lines are formatted including spacing, etc.

line indicator the indicator in the lower right-hand corner of the screen indicating line number

list files the WordPerfect feature that allows a listing of every file on a disk or directory and all the relevant information about when it was first created, its size, etc.

macro a set of keystrokes stored as a file

margins the defining edges of a document

math feature of WordPerfect that allows you to work with math tables, figures, listings, etc.

merge combining a primary and a secondary file to produce a new file, using merge commands

monitor the computer screen or terminal

move to move text from one place in a document to another place in the document or to another file

multiple tabs more than one tab on the same tab line

non-continuous double underlining underlining using double lines under individual words and not the spaces between them

non-continuous single underlining underlining using single lines under individual words and not the spaces between them

number pad the nine keys, usually on the right side, that have the numbers one to nine on them

outline a systematic set of statements that are all related to one another

output the results of your word processing efforts, usually in the form of a printed copy

page cursor movement movement of the cursor from page to page using the cursor keys

page format the way text on a page will appear

page indicator the indicator at the lower left-hand corner of the screen indicating the page number where the cursor is located in the active document

page length the number of lines on a printed page

page number position WordPerfect option that lets you decide where and how often you will number the pages of your document

page option option in which the page the cursor is on is printed

pagination the numbering of pages

pc an abbreviation for personal computer

personal dictionary the WordPerfect dictionary that you create by adding your own words that WordPerfect does not recognize

pica a typeface with ten characters per inch

preview option that allows you to view on the screen what the final printed document will actually look like

primary file the file in merging operations that "receives" the changing information; the letter that "receives" the different addresses

print the production of a hard copy

print format the way in which text is printed; options presented on the print format menu

print options menu list of the alternatives available for printing

printer the machine that prints a hard copy of a file

program disk the disk on which the program, WordPerfect, is stored

prompt a question or statement from the WordPerfect program requesting additional information or action of the user's part

RAM active memory in the computer that disappears when the computer is turned off

random access memory (RAM)

read the process through which the computer reads the information off of a disk

reformat change the physical appearance of a document, such as changing from 54 lines per page to 40 lines per page

rename renaming a file that already exists

replace to substitute one chain of characters for another

restore   take previously erased text and replace it in the document

retrieve   to recall an existing document and load it into the computer's RAM

reveal codes   the codes that indicate WordPerfect operations

reversal   text-entering error in which letters are reversed, as in "aep" for "ape"

revise   to edit and change for the next draft

right justify   to create an even right-hand edge on a document

right margin   the position along which the right-hand side of the text will be aligned

Roman numerals   I, II, III or i, ii, iii, iv

save   to record text on a floppy disk

screen cursor movement   movement of the cursor from one part of a screen to another using the cursor keys

screen dump   function that prints the exact contents of the screen, including the indicators at the bottom or top of the screen

screen down   to move the screen's contents one screen down on the monitor

screen up   to move the screen's contents one screen up on the monitor

search   to look for a string of characters

secondary file   the file in merging operations that is merged into a static primary file; the changing addresses into a letter

set-up menu   the menu that allows you to change WordPerfect default

skip   option in spell checker that tells WordPerfect that a word it doesn't recognize is spelled correctly and can be skipped the next time it appears

software   the directions that a computer needs to operate

spacing   the distance between lines

spell checker   the WordPerfect device that allows you to check and correct spelling errors

split screen   when two documents appear on the same screen

store   to save

string   a set of characters such as "this is" or "12, 23, 25, 23"

system level   the level of the operating system

tab   a preset stop for the cursor when the tab key is pressed

tab align   the Ctrl→F6 key, used in aligning characters

tab key   key that activates tabs

tab line   the indicator of where tabs are set

tab ruler   the line that indicates where margin settings and tabs are set

template   a guide to WordPerfect keys

top margin   the space between the top of the paper and the beginning of text

24 hour clock   time expressed on a 24 hour scale with 12 noon being 12:00 hours and midnight being 24:00 hours

typeover mode   the mode in which you can type over information rather than inserting it between characters

undelete   to undo the effects of a deletion

underline   to mark a straight line under a set of characters

window   the presentation of a document on part of the screen

word count   the number of words in a document

word cursor movement   movement of the cursor from word to word using the cursor keys

word pattern   A set of characters that WordPerfect can search for

word processor   an electronic tool that allows you to enter and manipulate text

word search   WordPerfect option that searches throughout a document for a specific group of characters

word wrap   automatic entry of words that don't fit on the previous lines

work disk   the disk on which files are stored

write when the computer wants to enter information

write protect sticker a sticker that prevents you from accidentally writing over an established file

WYSIWYG A "what you see is what you get" word processing quality, in which what appears on the screen is what will appear in the printed document

Quick Reference Chart for WordPerfect 4.2 Training Version

Use this chart when you want to know the exact set of key commands to begin a particular WordPerfect function. Remember, a right arrow like this

$$\rightarrow$$

means you should hold the first key down while you press the second. For example, to print a copy of a document, the command is

Shift→F7

which requires you to hold down the shift key while you press the F7 function key.

WordPerfect Feature	Key
Alignment Character	Shift→F8
Backspace	←
Block	Alt→F4
Block, Cut/Copy (Block on)	Ctrl→F4
Block Protect (Block on)	Alt→F8

WordPerfect Feature	Key
Bold	F6
Cancel	F1
Center	Shift→F6
Center Page Top to Bottom	Alt→F8
Change Directory	F5,7
Colors	Ctrl→F3
Column, Cut→Copy (Block on)	Ctrl→F4
Conditional End of Page	Ctrl→ <ret>
Copy (List Files)	F5,8
Date	Shift→F5
Delete	Del
Delete (List Files)	F5,2
Delete Directory (List Files)	F5,0
Delete to End of Line (EOL)	Ctrl→End
Delete to End of Page (EOP)	Ctrl→PgDn
Delete Word	Ctrl→Back Space
Enter (or Return)	<ret>
Escape	Esc
Exit	F7
Full Text (Print)	Shift→F7
Hard Page	Ctrl→<ret>
Hard Return	<ret>
Headers or Footers	Alt→F8
Help	F3
Hyphenation On/Off	Shift→F8,5
Justification On/Off	Ctrl→F8
Line Format	Shift→F8
List Files	F5,<ret>
Look	F5,6
Macro	Alt→F10
Macro Def	Ctrl→F10
Margins	Shift→F8
Merge	Ctrl→F9
Merge Codes	Alt→F9
Merge E	Shift→F9
Merge R	F9
Minus Sign	−
Move	Ctrl→F4
Name Search	F5,9
New Page Number	Alt→F4

Outline	Alt→F5
Page Format	Alt→F8
Page Length	Alt→F8
Page Number Column Positions	Alt→F8
Page Number Position	Alt,F8
Page (Print)	Shift→F7
Print	Shift→F7
Print (List Files)	F5,4
Print a Document	Shift→F7
Print Block (Block on)	Shift→F7
Print Format	Ctrl→F8
Rename (List Files)	F5,3
Retrieve	Shift→F10
Retrieve (List Files)	F5,1
Retrieve Text (Move)	Ctrl→F4
Reveal Codes	Alt→F3
Save	F10
Search Backward	Shift→F2
Search Forward	F2
Sort	Alt→F9
Sorting Sequences	Alt→F9
Spacing	Shift→F9
Spell	Ctrl→F2
Split Screen	Ctrl→F3,1
Switch Screens	Shift→F3
Tab	Tab
Tab Align	Ctrl→F6
Tab Ruler	Ctrl→F3,1
Tab Set	Shift→F8
Top Margin	Alt→F8
Typeover	Ins
Undelete	F1
Underline	F8
Underline Style	Ctrl→F8
Window	Ctrl→F3
Word Count	Ctrl→F2
Word Search	F5,9

WordPerfect Cursor Control

Beginning of Text arrow	Home, Home, up
End of Text arrow	Home, Home, down

WordPerfect Cursor Control

Line Left	Home, ←
Line Right	Home, →
Page Down	PgDn
Page Up	PgUp
Screen Down or +	Home, down arrow
Screen Up or −	Home, up arrow
Word Left	Ctrl ←
Word Right	Ctrl →

Reveal Codes

In lesson 12, you learned how *reveal codes* represent various WordPerfect operations (such as blocking) and document characteristics (such as spacing and margin adjustments). Here is the complete list of all the reveal codes that will ever appear in a WordPerfect document when the Alt→F3 key combination is pressed. Although many of these operations are discussed throughout *Mastering WordPerfect*, it is beyond the scope of this book to cover them all.

Code	Action
[^](blinking)	Cursor Position
[]	Hard Space
[-]	Hyphen
-(blinking)	Soft Hyphen
[A][a]	Tab Align or Flush Right
[Adv]	Advance Up 1/2 Line
[Adv]	Advance Down 1/2 Line
[AdvLn:n]	Advance to Specific Line Number
[Align Char:]	Alignment Character
[B][b]	Bold (begin and end)
[Block]	Beginning of Block
[BlockPro:Off]	Block Protection off
[BlockPro:On]	Block Protection on
[C][c]	Centering (begin and end)
[Center Pg]	Center Current Page Top to Bottom
[Cmnd:]	Embedded Printer Command
[Col Def:]	Column Definition
[Col Off]	End of Text Columns

Code	*Action*
[Col On]	Beginning of Text Columns
[Date:n]	Date/Time function (n = format)
[DefMark:Index,n]	Index Definition (n = format)
[DefMark:List,n]	List Definition (n = List Number)
[DefMark:ToC,n]	Table of Contents Definition
[EInd]	End of Indent or Indent
[EndDef]	End of Index, List, or Table of Contents
[EndMark:List,n]	End Marked Text (n = List Number)
[EndMark:ToC,n]	End Marked Text (n = ToC Level)
[E-Tabs:n,n]	Extended Tabs (begin with n, every n spaces)
[Font Change:n,n]	Specify New Font or Print Wheel
[FtnOpt]	Footnote/Endnote Options
[Hdr/Ftr:n,ntext]	Header or Footer Definition
[HPg]	Hard Page
[HRt]	Hard Return
[Hyph on]	Hyphenation on
[Hyph off]	Hyphenation off
[HZone Set:n,n]	Reset Size of Hyphenation Zone
[Indent]	Beginning of Indent
[Indent]	Beginning of Left/Right Indent
[Index:heading; subheading]	Index Mark
[LPI:n]	Lines per Inch
[Mar Rel:n]	Left Margin Release
[Margin Set:n,n]	Left and Right Margin Reset
[Mark:List,n]	Begin Marked Text for List
[Mark:ToC,n]	Begin Marked Text for ToC
[Math Def]	Definition of Math Columns
[Math Off]	End of Math
[Math On]	Beginning of Math
!(blinking)	Formula Calculation
t(blinking)	Subtotal Entry
+(blinking)	Do Subtotal
T(blinking)	Total Entry
=(blinking)	Do Total
*(blinking)	Do Grand Total
[Note:End, n;[note#]text]	Endnote (n = Endnote Number)
[Note:Foot, n;[note#]text]	Footnote (n = Footnote Number)

[Ovrstk]	Overstrike Preceding Character
[Par#:Auto]	Automatic Paragraph/Outline Number
[Par#:n]	Fixed Paragraph Number (n = level number)
[Par#Def]	Paragraph Numbering Definition
[Pg#:n]	New Page Number
[Pg#Col:n,n,n]	Column Position for Page Numbers (n= left, center, right)
[PgLnth:n,n]	Set Page Length (n = form lines, text lines)
[PosPg#:n]	Set Position for Page Numbers
[RedLn][r]	Redline (begin and end)
[Rt Just Off]	Right Justification off
[Rt Just On]	Right Justification on
[Set Ftn#:n]	New Footnote Number
[Spacing Set:n]	Spacing Set
[SPg]	Soft New Page
[SRt]	Soft Return
[StrkOut][s]	Strikeout (begin and end)
[SubScrpt]	Subscript
[SuprScrpt]	Superscript
[Suppress:n]	Suppress Page Format Options (n = format(s))
[TAB]	Move to Next Tab Stop
[Tab Set:]	Tab Reset
[Top Mar:n]	Set Top Margin in Half-Lines
[U][u]	Underlining (begin and end)
[Undrl Style:n]	Underline Style
[W/O Off]	Widow/Orphan Off
[W/O On]	Widow/Orphan On

The WordPerfect Set-up Menu

When you first started using WordPerfect and writing the memo in lesson 3, certain characteristics of the program were preset. For example, without any special directions from you, WordPerfect automatically knows to place only one space between lines. Also, the margin for the left side of the document was set at 10 spaces and the margin for the right side was set at 74 spaces.

These are only two examples of the many *default* settings that WordPerfect has preset for you. A default setting is the setting that the program will always return to and use unless given other directions. In other words, unless you tell WordPerfect, it will always place only one space between lines and have margins set at 10 and 74.

Although having these WordPerfect features preset can be very convenient, you may need to change some of them to better fit your work habits and the way you use WordPerfect. You make changes in the default features of WordPerfect with the *set-up menu*.

Permanent versus Temporary Changes

There are actually two ways to make changes to the WordPerfect settings. The first way is with the set-up menu. Here, you can change WordPerfect default settings so that every time you start WordPerfect, these new settings will be active. These are *permanent* changes. They will stay in force until you change the default values on the set-up menu again.

For example, if you always type documents that are double spaced, you might want to change the default spacing setting to 2 from the current default setting of 1. There are times however, when you might want to change the spacing to one line for only *part* of a document. For example,

> quotations are usually single-spaced, when the rest of a manuscript is double-spaced. WordPerfect allows you to change the spacing (as well as many other features) from *inside* the document itself.

In this case, the only thing that will be affected is the document you are working on, and not future WordPerfect files. This is an example of a *temporary* change.

Which of these two strategies is better for you? In general, as you go through the set-up procedure that follows, change only those default settings that you are sure you would want changed *every time* you sit down to work with WordPerfect.

Why Should I Change Anything?

An excellent question and one worth taking a moment to answer. Many WordPerfect users don't have "special" requirements concerning such things as spacing, format, or other default settings. If you don't need to change any settings, don't feel that you have to. WordPerfect can operate nicely without any changes to the set-up menu. Also, it may take you some time to fully understand all the available options and which you may want to change.

Read this section of WordPerfect Extras to learn what options are available if you should want to make "permanent" changes to the default settings at any time and how you can change them.

Starting WordPerfect All Over Again

In order to examine or reset any of the default settings, you have to "start" WordPerfect all over. To leave WordPerfect and start the set-up menu, do the following.

1. Press the F7 key and save whatever is on your WordPerfect screen.

2. When you are asked, "Exit WordPerfect?," enter the letter Y. These two steps should return you to the system level where you will see the A prompt (A>).

3. To start the set-up menu, type in A>wp/s <ret>. You may recognize that this is the same command you used to start WordPerfect, but with a slash (/) and an "s" added on. This command calls up the WordPerfect set-up menu and the set-up routine.

The first screen you will see after you type in this command is the WordPerfect welcome screen. After you "Press any key to continue", you should see the screen shown in figure A–1, which is the WordPerfect set-up menu.

The WordPerfect Set-Up Menu

As you can see in figure A–1, there are four categories of Word-Perfect settings that can be changed.

Setting Directories allows you to tell WordPerfect where (on what disk drive) information on the WordPerfect speller and the-saurus will be stored.

Set Initial Settings deals with many different settings such as the length of the page, the margin settings, where page numbers will appear on the screen, and more.

Set Screen Size allows you to adjust the number of rows and columns that show on the screen.

```
                           Set-up Menu

          0 - End Set-up and enter WP

          1 - Set Directories or Drives for Dictionary and Thesaurus Files
          2 - Set Initial Settings
          3 - Set Screen and Beep Options
          4 - Set Backup Options

          Selection:

          Press Cancel to ignore changes and return to DOS
```

Figure A–1   The WordPerfect Set-up Menu

Set Backup Options allows you to do two things. The first is to
have WordPerfect automatically backup the file that you are working on with a specified amount of time between automatic backups.
Second, you can choose whether or not to have WordPerfect do a
backup of the original file.

Here's a more detailed description of these different options.

Setting the Spelling and Dictionary Directories

When you set up WordPerfect for your everyday use, one of the
things you need to do is to indicate *where,* or in what file, the spelling feature can be found or reside. In other words, you need to tell
WordPerfect where to look (or in what directory) to find the information that it needs. As you have already seen, although Word-
Perfect offers a thesaurus as well as a speller, *Mastering Word-
Perfect* only covers the speller.

The three files are the *dictionary* (named LEX.WordPerfect),
which contains words used by the spell checker to help you correct
misspellings; the *supplementary dictionary,* which will contain
words that you learned how to add to WordPerfect's existing dic-

```
                          Set-up Menu

      0 - End Set-up and enter WP

      1 - Set Directories or Drives for Dictionary and Thesaurus Files
      2 - Set Initial Settings
      3 - Set Screen and Beep Options
      4 - Set Backup Options

      Selection:

      Where do you plan to keep the dictionary (LEX.WP)?
      Enter full pathname: A:\LEX.WP
```

Figure A–2   Storing Locations

tionary (using option 3 on the speller menu); and the *thesaurus* (named TH.WordPerfect on your disk). A thesaurus is a dictionary of synonyms that can be used to substitute for other words.

When you choose option 1 on the set-up menu, you will see the screen in figure A–2. You need to indicate the disk drive where you plan on keeping the dictionary, the supplemental dictionary, and the thesaurus. In general, these files will reside on your WordPerfect program disk, which is located in drive A.

When you are asked to enter the full *path* name, type **a:** <ret>. A path is a direction that the operating system uses to find a file. In this case, you are telling WordPerfect that the files can be found at the end of the path that is reached through the **a:** command.

Enter this command for each of the three different questions. After you have entered the path for the third and last time and pressed the return key, you will be returned to the set-up menu in figure A–1. When you are finished with this part of the set-up menu, WordPerfect will know where to find the dictionary and the supplemental dictionary.

```
Change Initial Settings

Press any of the keys listed below to change initial settings

Key                Initial Settings

Line Format        Tabs, Margins, Spacing, Hyphenation, Align Character
Page Format        Page # Pos, Page Length, Top Margin, Page # Col Pos, W/O
Print Format       Pitch, Font, Lines/Inch, Right Just, Underlining, SF Bin #
Print              Printer, Copies, Binding Width
Date               Date Format
Insert/Typeover    Insert/Typeover Mode
Mark Text          Paragraph Number Definition, Table of Authorities Definition
Footnote           Footnote/Endnote Options
Escape             Set N
Screen             Set Auto-rewrite
Text In/Out        Set Insert Document Summary on Save/Exit

Selection:

Press Enter to return to the Set-up Menu
```

Figure A–3   Setting Initial WordPerfect Settings

Setting Initial Settings

The next group of settings you will address, shown in figure A–3, are changed by selecting option 2 on the set-up menu.

The general category of these features and what each one does is as follows.

Line Format. Changes the appearance of individual lines, such as spacing and margins.

Page Format. Changes the appearance of individual pages such as the position of the page number, how long the page is, and so forth.

Print Format. Changes the style of underlining, number of lines printed per inch, justification, and more.

Print. Deals with the number of copies to be printed, and more.

Date. Determines the format of how the date appears on your monitor, such as March 4, 1987 or 3-4-87.

Insert/Typeover. Determines whether your input will "type over" what is there or be inserted.

Mark Text. Helps you in defining and numbering paragraphs.

Footnote. Provides you with the footnote and endnote options that are available in WordPerfect.

Escape. Allows you to move lines or spaces a set number of times.

Screen. Provides you with the option to have WordPerfect automatically change the document on your screen as you save changes from the keyboard. This is called *auto-rewrite.* For example, if you change the spacing, with the rewrite option on, the change in spacing will be shown throughout the entire document.

It's very important to remember that if you are comfortable with WordPerfect as a word processing program, it's probably best to leave these default settings alone. Remember, you can always change a WordPerfect feature such as spacing or the way the date is printed, for any *one* document and these changes will be in force *only* for that one document.

If you change a default value on the set-up menu, that change will remain and be in force each time you load WordPerfect. If you want to change it then, you have to return to the set-up menu and reset the default value. For example, when working with the set-up menu, you can set WordPerfect so that

> every time you begin
> using the program,
> the margins will be
> set at 10 and 30, and
> the lines will be
> single spaced,
> perfect for a
> newsletter column.

This kind of permanent change is too drastic a step since it means that *everything* you do in WordPerfect will appear as a single-spaced column with these margins. A more realistic approach is to experiment with WordPerfect and find out what you want to keep as is and what you might like to change.

For example, if you wanted your documents to be double spaced most of the time, you need to change the default of 1 to 2. How would you do this? You can see in figure A–3 that the key that deals with changing spacing is Line Format, which corresponds to the combination of the Shift→F8 keys. Once this combination of

```
Change Initial Settings

Press any of the keys listed below to change initial settings

Key               Initial Settings

Line Format       Tabs, Margins, Spacing, Hyphenation, Align Character
Page Format       Page # Pos, Page Length, Top Margin, Page # Col Pos, W/O
Print Format      Pitch, Font, Lines/Inch, Right Just, Underlining, SF Bin #
Print             Printer, Copies, Binding Width
Date              Date Format
Insert/Typeover   Insert/Typeover Mode
Mark Text         Paragraph Number Definition, Table of Authorities Definition
Footnote          Footnote/Endnote Options
Escape            Set N
Screen            Set Auto-rewrite
Text In/Out       Set Insert Document Summary on Save/Exit

Selection:

Press Enter to return to the Set-up Menu


1 2 Tabs; 3 Margins; 4 Spacing; 5 Hyphenation; 6 Align Char: 0
```

Figure A–4   Changing the Spacing

keys is pressed, a new line will appear on the bottom of your screen, as shown in figure A–4.

This is the same menu you saw in figure 13–1. The only difference here is that the changes are permanent (until reset once again). In this example, spacing will change, so select option 3. When this is done, you will see (as in figure A–5), at the lower left-hand corner of the screen, a message that the current spacing is set at 1 space. To change this value, simply type in whatever number of spaces you want and press the return key.

Until you are sure that you want it to be otherwise, it is best to leave the spacing at 1 line, which is the most convenient set-up for letters and such. Besides, you can change the spacing for a particular document as needed.

Setting the Screen Size

The next item on the set-up menu is *screen size*, or the number of rows and columns that you want on your monitor. As you can see in figure A–6, most computers operate with 80 columns and 24 lines *on any one screen*. If you should want to change these settings, just type in the new values and press the return key.

```
Change Initial Settings

Press any of the keys listed below to change initial settings

Key              Initial Settings

Line Format      Tabs, Margins, Spacing, Hyphenation, Align Character
Page Format      Page # Pos, Page Length, Top Margin, Page # Col Pos, W/O
Print Format     Pitch, Font, Lines/Inch, Right Just, Underlining, SF Bin #
Print            Printer, Copies, Binding Width
Date             Date Format
Insert/Typeover  Insert/Typeover Mode
Mark Text        Paragraph Number Definition, Table of Authorities Definition
Footnote         Footnote/Endnote Options
Escape           Set N
Screen           Set Auto-rewrite
Text In/Out      Set Insert Document Summary on Save/Exit

Selection:

Press Enter to return to the Set-up Menu


[Spacing Set] 1
```

Figure A–5   Single Spacing

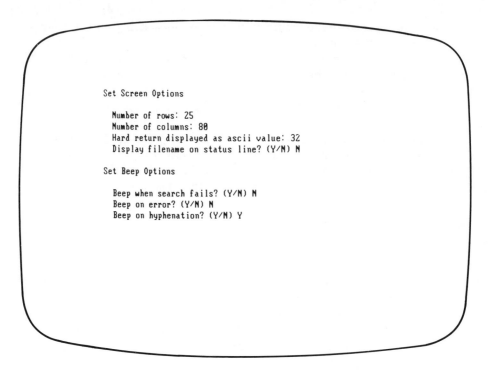

```
Set Screen Options

    Number of rows: 25
    Number of columns: 80
    Hard return displayed as ascii value: 32
    Display filename on status line? (Y/N) N

Set Beep Options

    Beep when search fails? (Y/N) N
    Beep on error? (Y/N) N
    Beep on hyphenation? (Y/N) Y
```

Figure A–6   Screen–Size Settings

Setting Backup Instructions

One of the most important and valuable features of any word processor, and WordPerfect is no exception, is the *backup* feature. This is the last item on the original set-up menu as shown in figure A–7.

As you can see, you have two different questions to answer. The first asks whether you want to *automatically* have *timed backups* made as you work. If so, you are to enter the number of minutes that you want to pass between each backup.

Timed backups are very convenient. The only disadvantage is that right in the middle of your working the computer will begin backing up the file that you are working on, and you will have to wait until it is finished.

The second option will create an extra backup copy of your file and rename it, giving it the extension ".BK!". So if you write a letter for a friend and save the file as "michael.ltr", WordPerfect will automatically save it as "michael.bk!"

When asked if you want to back up the original, type in the

```
Set Timed Backup

To safeguard against losing large amounts of text in the event of a power or
machine failure, WordPerfect can automatically backup the document on your
screen at a chosen time interval and to a chosen drive/directory (see Set-up
in the WordPerfect Installation pamphlet).  REMEMBER--THIS IS ONLY IN CASE OF
POWER OR MACHINE FAILURE.  WORDPERFECT DELETES THE TIMED BACKUP FILES WHEN YOU
EXIT NORMALLY FROM WORDPERFECT.  If you want the document saved as a file you
need to say 'yes' when you exit WordPerfect normally.

Number of minutes between each backup: 0


Set Original Backup

WordPerfect can rename the last copy of a document when a new version of the
document is saved.  The old copy has the same file name with an extension of
".BK!".  Take note that the files named "letter.1" and "letter.2" have the
same original backup file name of "letter.bk!".  In this case the latest
file saved will be backed up.

Backup the original document? (Y/N) N
```

Figure A–7   Backup Settings

letter Y and press the return. You will be returned to the opening
set-up screen shown in figure A–1.

Leaving the WordPerfect Set-Up Menu

When you are satisfied that you have made the changes you want
in the default settings, and you have been returned to the screen
shown in figure A–1 (the opening set-up screen), press the 0 key
and the changes you made will be recorded and you will be placed
directly into WordPerfect. Every time that you begin WordPerfect,
any settings you have changed will be in place.

Index

WordPerfect
C O R P O R A T I O N

School Software Direct Order Form

Qualifying teachers, as well as college, university, and other post-secondary students, can now purchase WordPerfect Corporation (WPCORP) software directly from WPCORP at a reduced price. To qualify, a participant must be teaching or currently enrolled as a full-time student, and must agree in writing not to resell or transfer any package purchased under this program.

If you satisfy these qualifying conditions and would like to purchase software directly from WPCORP under the School Software Program, complete the following six steps and sign at the bottom of the form.

Step 1. From the list below, select the appropriate software for your computer (please note that each student is limited to *one* package of WordPerfect) and mark an "x" in the corresponding box(es).

Product	Disk Size	Computer	Price*
☐ WordPerfect 4.2	5¼"	(IBM PC/XT/AT/Compatibles)	$125.00
☐ WordPerfect 4.2	3½"	(IBM PC/XT/AT/compatibles)	125.00
☐ WordPerfect 1.1	5¼"	(Apple IIe/IIc)	59.00
☐ WordPerfect 1.1	3½"	(Apple IIe/IIc)	59.00
☐ WordPerfect 1.1	3½"	(Apple IIGS)	59.00
☐ PlanPerfect 3.0	5¼"	(IBM PC/XT/AT/Compatibles)	99.00
☐ PlanPerfect 3.0	3½"	(IBM PC/XT/AT/Compatibles)	99.00
☐ WordPerfect Library	5¼"	(IBM PC/XT/AT/Compatibles)	59.00
☐ WordPerfect Library	3½"	(IBM PC/XT/AT/Compatibles)	59.00
☐ WordPerfect Executive	5¼"	(IBM PC/XT/AT/Compatibles)	79.00
☐ WordPerfect Executive	3½"	(IBM PC/XT/AT/Compatibles)	79.00

Step 2. Make a photo-copy of your current Student ID or Faculty card *and* a photo-copy of some well known form of identification displaying your social security number, such as your Driver License or Social Security Card. (WPCORP will hold this information strictly confidential and use it only to guard against duplicate purchases.) Your school ID must show current enrollment. If it does not show a date, you must send verification of current enrollment. If you have serious reservations about providing a social security number, call Educational Development at (801) 227-7131 to establish clearance to purchase any of the above software products at these special prices.

Step 3. Enter your social security number: ___ ___ ___ – ___ ___ – ___ ___ ___ ___ .

Step 4. Enclose payment for the total cost of the package(s) ordered with personal check, money order, Visa, or MasterCard.

Account # _____

Expiration Date _____ ☐ VISA   ☐ MasterCard

(Make check or money order payable to WordPerfect Corporation.)

Step 5. List your shipping address and the address of your local computer store (dealer) in the space provided:

Ship To _____ Your Dealer _____

_____ _____

_____ _____

Phone _____ Phone _____

Step 6. Enclose this signed and completed form, the photo-copies of your identification cards, and your signed check or money order (or Visa or MasterCard account number and expiration date) in an envelope and mail to School Software Program, WordPerfect Corporation, 288 West Center Street, Orem, UT 84057.

The information provided herein is correct and accurate, and I will abide by the restricting conditions outlined by WPCORP in this document. I understand that at its sole discretion, WPCORP may refuse any order for any reason.

Signature _____ Date _____

*Utah residents add 6.25% sales tax.

MEMO

TO: Users of the Limited-Use version of WordPerfect 4.2
FROM: WordPerfect Corporation
RE: The limitations of Limited-Use WordPerfect 4.2
DATE: June 30, 1987
****

The Limited-Use introductory version of WordPerfect 4.2 (L-WP) is intended to allow one to *learn* the features of WordPerfect 4.2; however, the L-WP is not intended to allow one to print usable academic or professional documents[1].

Certain limitations (*which should not deter learning WordPerfect through the L-WP*) have been encrypted into the L-WP to guard against productive use, and are as follows:

I.   One may work with as large a document on screen as desired, but one may only save to disk a data file no larger than 50,000k (appx. 25-30 regular pages).

            1.   A data file created with the L-WP cannot be imported into regular WordPerfect, nor can a file created in regular WordPerfect be imported into L-WP.

II.   Data files of any size may be printed through parallel printer port "1" without defining a printer, but font changes and extended ASCII characters are not allowed. Also, "**WPC**" will be printed after each paragraph.

III.   One will be able to learn all the functions of WordPerfect 4.2's speller and thesaurus by calling up the "readme.wp" file and following the step-by-step directions; however, one cannot use the L-WP speller and thesaurus with any of one's own documents because there are only a limited number of words in the L-WP speller and thesaurus. (The regular speller has 115,000 words, and the regular thesaurus has approximately 150,000 words.)

IV.   The help file of L-WP allows the user to retrieve the function-key template, but similar to the speller and the thesaurus described above, space will not allow the full help files on the L-WP disk.

L-WP is designed to be used for introductory, word processing courses, and thus far has been well received in these types of environments.
Notwithstanding the broad abilities provided in the L-WP, presumably the L-WP will not satisfactorily substitute for regular WordPerfect 4.2, and therefore the full feature version may be obtained directly from WordPerfect Corporation via the enclosed order form at a 75% educational discount.

---

[1]"**WPC**" will be automatically printed after each paragraph of text to discourage academic or professional use of the L-WP. *See* paragraph II above.

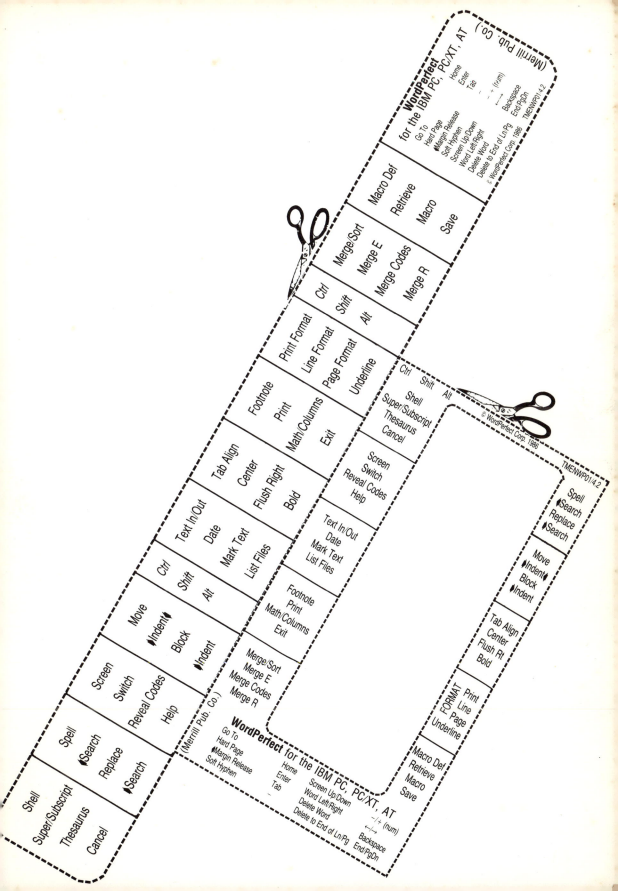

WordPerfect for the IBM PC, PC/XT, AT (Merrill Pub. Co.)

Go To Hard Page ◄Margin Release Soft Hyphen Screen Up/Down Word Left/Right Delete Word Delete to End of Ln/Pg

Home Enter Tab -/+ (num) Backspace End/PgDn

© WordPerfect Corp. 1986 TMENWP01/4.2

Ctrl	Shift	Alt
Macro Def	Merge/Sort	Print Format
Retrieve	Merge E	Line Format
Macro	Merge Codes	Page Format
Save	Merge R	Underline

Footnote	Tab Align	Text In/Out
Print	Center	Date
Math/Columns	Flush Right	Mark Text
Exit	Bold	List Files

Ctrl	Shift	Alt
Move	Screen	Spell
◄Indent►	Switch	◄Search
Block	Reveal Codes	Replace
◄Indent	Help	Search►

Shell
Super/Subscript
Thesaurus
Cancel

Ctrl	Shift	Alt
Shell	Screen	Spell
Super/Subscript	Switch	◄Search
Thesaurus	Reveal Codes	Replace
Cancel	Help	◄Search

Text In/Out	Move	
Date	◄Indent►	
Mark Text	Block	
List Files	◄Indent	

Footnote	FORMAT Print	Tab Align
Print	Line	Center
Math/Columns	Page	Flush Rt
Exit	Underline	Bold

Merge/Sort	Macro Def
Merge E	Retrieve
Merge Codes	Macro
Merge R	Save

WordPerfect for the IBM PC, PC/XT, AT (Merrill Pub. Co.)

Go To Hard Page ◄Margin Release Soft Hyphen

Home Enter Tab Screen Up/Down Word Left/Right Delete Word Delete to End of Ln/Pg -/+ (num) Backspace End/PgDn

TMENWP01/4.2